Wojciech 'Nathaniel' Usarzewicz

NATHANIEL

PSYCHIC DEVELOPMENT SIMPLIFIED

Third Edition

Copyright © 2010, 2011 Wojciech 'Nathaniel' Usarzewicz

All rights reserved, including the right to reproduce this work in any form whatsoever, without permission in writing from the author, except for brief passages in connection with a review.

This book is being distributed on-line, through A State of Mind, supported by E-Junkie, Lulu.com and Amazon.com.

Published by A State of Mind, Wroclaw 2011, Poland
Design and DTP by Nathaniel
Website: http://astateofmind.eu
Printed through CreateSpace.

ISBN 978-1466414266

Self-publishing effort by non-native English speaker. Grammar and spelling edit with help of Grammarly software. Please report any grammar and/or spelling errors to: *nathan@astateofmind.eu*

Additional Credit:
A State of Mind's Logo Font – Fertigo, by
http://exljbris.com/fertigo.html
Other cover fonts include: Optimus Princeps by Manfred Klein
Floral elements by SugarBreezy:
http://sugarbreezy.deviantart.com/

Disclaimer

All information included in this e-book represents the author's point of view. Author of this work does not take responsibility for any physical or mental damage caused by use of the exercises within this e-book. Author wish to inform that all practical exercises from this book has been tested on his own skin, and he's still alive to share experiences and knowledge.

Thanks to...

I want to thank guys behind the PsiOps game for helping me become interested in psychic phenomena. Thanks to Jennifer Brown for writing Playful Psychic and to Sean Connelly for creating PsiPog.net; Chris for creating United Psionics Club; Robert Bruce for publishing his book about energy work; Debra Katz for proving my abilities (even if she don't know who the heck I am) by writing her own book on psychic development where she wrote everything I have found out myself; Maurio McKay for still commenting on my Facebook page; Sarah Spock from PsionicsOnline.net for inspiring me without even realizing it; and finally readers of A State of Mind and followers on Twitter, especially Courtney Mroch from Haunt Jaunts - you all rock!

Very, very special thanks to Anette, her smile make my life beautiful day by day!

Table of Contents

Psychics Surround Us..........................10
Who Is Psychic, Anyway?........................15
How Psychic Do You Want To Become..............23
First Step in Working Out Your Blockages.......32
Short History Of Psychic Development...........39

The Essence Of Theory........................42
Psychic Energies...............................43
Chakras..53

The Mind Work................................67
Meditation.....................................67
Other Ways Of Dealing With Blockages...........83
Intuition......................................89
Affirmations...................................95
Emotional Healing Work........................103

Safe Psychic...............................114

Breathe & Attraction.......................118
Throat Chakra Breathing.......................120
Heng Haa Breath...............................121
Psychic Shaping Life..........................123

New Energy Ways............................131
Energy Theory.................................134
New Energy Ways - Developing Energy System....138

Psychic Arts...............................155
Psychic Field Maintenance.....................156

Opening & Balancing Chakras................163
Chakra Stimulation............................165

Psychic Work..173

How To Sense Energy..174
Creating A Psiball..176
Visualization...182
Psychic Self-Defense...183
Psychic Attacks...192

Extra Sensory Perception........................198

Different Forms Of Psychic Perception................................200
Aura View..204
Psychic Reading..210
Psychometry...224
Telepathy...228
Art of Remote Viewing..229
Precognition and Dreams..237
Empathy..238

Advanced Energy Work............................240

Psychic Healing..240
Telekinesis...244

Last, But Not Least...................................252

Pendulums And Rods..252
Crystals In Psychic Work..258
World Of Skeptic..261
The World Of Spirits...269
Channeling...271
The Book Of Exercises..272
Moving Further..278
Summary of the book..280

Resources...281

Glossary of Terms...284
Bibliography and further reading...288

Introduction To Third Edition

Psychic Development Simplified came a long way from the first to the third edition. From little over 100 pages, the length of the book reached over 250 pages, and a lot of training material has been added to make sure you get the best psychic development guide ever. From a bit 'psipunk' work for psychic wannabes, Psychic Development Simplified became a guide to both psychic and spiritual growth.

A lot have happened in the past year, since I published the first edition of this book. New knowledge, new understanding, and new point of view have led me to reworking my bestselling book. Now, the third edition creates even better psychic development workbook, once again presenting things with as simple words as possible.

The main difference between 2nd edition and 3rd edition is that I've added a whole section about advanced mind-work: affirmations and emotional healing. My current understanding is simple: energy work + meditation + mind work can turn you into a psychic even faster than before. If you have read any of the previous editions, then know this: core of the book is still energy work and step-by-step tutorials. I've just expanded the knowledge further.

I've spent a lot of time making sure that my grammar will prove to be of as greatest quality as possible. Yet, I hope that you will understand that I'm not a native English speaker, and that this book is a result of self-publishing effort. But even so, even if my English isn't perfect, I still want to share knowledge with as many people as possible. And publishing in English is the best way to do so.

I hope you will find this book useful in your psychic pursuits. And if you do (or if you don't), don't hesitate to send me your feedback, testimonials and reviews, so I can improve this work even further. Send your opinions to nathan@astateofmind.eu.

Psychics Surround Us

"What one has not experienced, one will never understand in print." - Isadora Duncan

The world of the supernatural is quite fascinating - from psychic phenomena to cryptozoology (scientific and semi-scientific studies meant to discover yet unknown species), from UFO to conspiracy theories. For some people such as myself, the paranormal and the occult are the fields of our human existence that are yet to be explored and understood. We, as those who explore these fields of knowledge, are pioneers, we are the first to experiment, first to understand, and although the science behind supernatural is nearly 200 years old already, and the knowledge towards understanding. And we do explore the supernatural because we want to understand.

Some of us want to understand why people reports paranormal experiences all around the world. And some people, such as myself, want to understand the reasons behind specific phenomena they have experienced at some point of life. I can remember my first encounter with poltergeist, when I was thrown onto a wall. I can remember seeing the spirit of my dad in the day of his funeral. I can remember the spirit pushing me when I paid a visit to a haunted flat during one of my paranormal investigations. I can remember bending spoons by accident and being unable to repeat the process, having precognitive dreams or knowing things before they happen on a daily basis. That's why for years, I was interested in the field of paranormal. I looked for answers. Today, I search illumination, and I want to share my knowledge. I have found all the answers I wanted, and even if I still do paranormal investigations these days, my primary goal is to share my knowledge, and use my skills to help people.

Some people prefer to use scientific knowledge and technology in their paranormal research. I prefer to use my psychic abilities. Abilities, which I have learned from scratches in last few years. After years of studies and practice, I have become psychic, and that's why you're holding this book. Because you want to become psychic, as well.

This book is a result of my own personal exploration that begun around year 2004. I started by reading a website - PsiPog.net, an on-line portal dedicated to "psionics". Psionics was a mixture of scientific approach and spiritual techniques of the East, a system of psychic development quite popular in the years 1995-2005, especially among Internet users. Next, I moved from PsiPog.net to other websites, from which I moved to books, and then even more books. It's funny, because what school failed to teach me, psychic development and interest in esoteric arts did – I have fallen in love with books.

I tried Anka's Energy Work techniques, Bronnikov's Method, New Energy Ways (also known as NEW). Today I practice the art of Tai Chi Chuan, as well. I have become Reiki practitioner, and that gave me additional boost for my own development.

Having hundreds of hours of learning and experiencing things behind me, it's time to share knowledge with those, who seek it. Because I love writing, I thought that writing this book will be the best way to share what I have learned. Or maybe it's my small psychic ego, as having your own book on the shelf, that sounds pretty cool. So here I am, listening to AC/DC, enjoying my coffee, and writing the workbook of psychic development.

I have decided to write this book because I wanted to collect all my current knowledge about basics of psychic development in one place, and teach others what I know. Finally, this book is meant to give people inspiration to start exploration of the supernatural on their own, by teaching where more knowledge can be found and how to keep yourself motivated. I hope you will find this book helpful.

In a way, this book is meant for me – as a chronicle of my own practical exploration, and current understanding of psychic phenomena. As such, it will also serve you well. I can't think of a better way of teaching others than teaching them everything I have learned.

Within this book, I have included as much information about basics of psychic development as I thought will be appropriate - here I discuss energy work and theory of psychic energies; basic energy manipulation, creation of psiballs and programming of psychic constructs; extra-sensory perception and ways of giving psychic reading and performing psychometry session, all of this are the very basics of psychic abilities one should learn about when thinking about moving forward. Finally, at the end of the book you will find a glossary of terms and information about further reading. But this is just the beginning, of course, as psychic phenomena is much wider than ESP. It's a way of living, from diet to making money and such. Don't be surprised as I have included a section about the famous law of attraction within this book. But one thing at the time.

This book should be consider to be a workbook - it contains practical knowledge and schedules meant to help you develop your psychic abilities from scratches. It also contains theory, but this theory is meant only for better understanding of the practical psychic phenomena. This book is not meant to explain psychic phenomena, provide proofs and explanations, but to provide you with guidelines and tips for your own psychic development. It does that by providing you with exercises and schedules supported with theory and personal experiences of the author.

So, You Want To Be Psychic?

So you want to be psychic. Actually, the truth is that you are psychic already, but you're not tuned into your psychic senses, yet. Unless you're natural psychic and you have bought this book just to learn few additional things. The main goal of this book is to awake your inner psychic 'self', so you can become aware of the energies and information flowing all around you. For many years, I was teaching people how to unleash their psychic potential through my website, A State of Mind. Yet by providing them with books and articles on the subject, I have learned that it is time to re-think the whole "awakening" thing, and rebuild it into a new book. Thus, the third edition of Psychic Development Simplified was created.

Also, this book has been designed to provide information for both total newbies, and natural psychics as well – people who were born with awaken psychic abilities. This is how things look like, everyone is born psychic. But later on, because of socialization and living in the Western world, people lose their abilities, and they forget how to use them. But some people remain psychics to some degree. You might be such born, natural psychic. You might already experience some psychic phenomena around you. For example, you might sense the presence of spirits, or you might know things before they happen, or you might see auras and so on). This book has been designed in such way, so born psychic on any level is still provided with useful information that can help him learn more control over his abilities.

Everyone is psychic. This statement hasn't changed a bit since I wrote Psychic Development Simplified for the first time. But everyone is a psychic to some degree, everyone have a limit of belief. This limit is like a borderline, whatever lies beyond it, is unacceptable for the person and in most cases is either ignored, or never really perceived by your brain. Turning from an ordinary person to psychic is based upon both energy work and mind work - you need to work with energies in order to prepare your physical and etherical bodies for psychic work, and you need to work with your mind in order to allow yourself to perceive this mystical world of psychic phenomena.

Did you know that when Christopher Columbus arrived to the new world, the natives were unable to see the ships? It was up to the shaman to notice the ripples on the water, where the ships were anchored. He was standing on the shore, looking for days, until he managed to see the ships. It's not just a funny story, but it is a truth. This is how our brain works. If you cannot accept something, or you're not aware that something is possible, your brain will either hide it, or deny it, or change it into something that looks familiar to you. It's how things look like, and you can't change it. That's why Zen practice is meant to teach how to see the world as it truly is. Because everything you see is just an illusion, created by your brain. Becoming psychic, awakening your psychic abilities is nothing else, but removing these brain filters that won't allow you to see the real world. And this can be achieved by energy work and by mind work.

Who Is Psychic, Anyway?

Before we start digging into practical exercises, affirmations, healing emotions, meditation and energy work, you must first learn who is a psychic, and what you should truly expect from this book, or any psychic development book, course or workshop. First of all, no psychic is X-Man, and we can't throw people onto walls. Believe it or not, but a lot of especially young people think that they can become such X-Man-like psychics, and it's their primary motivation for psychic development. I could describe psychics with details, yet it will be much simpler when, instead of general descriptions, I will describe four people who are psychics – me, and three other persons.

- **Martha** - She's a lawyer, and she's psychic, because she can sense and read people. You can simple enter her office, and within seconds, she will know that you're either guilty or not, or that you're going to pay for her services or not. It's very useful ability in her skill, but it's just the beginning. Because she's highly intuitive, she just knows which clients should she pick, and which cases should she drop, it's good for business. Her ability can be defined simple by "knowing things".
- **Tom** - While Martha can read people, Tom can see spirits – literally. And he can talk to them, so he can help them finish their unfinished earthly businesses and move on to the Light. This is the classic type of psychic known from TV. I guess you could call him a medium.

- **Geena** - Geena is energy healer. She's using her intuition and energy work abilities to heal people on the etherical, emotional and mental level. Therefore, she is able to heal physical illnesses, as well.
- **Myself** - I have the ability to perceive chakras and energetic bodies through clairvoyant vision, so I can advice you in many aspects of your life, from relationships to business, from psychic development to spiritual growth. Because I'm a trained psychic and I focus on continuing development, I also do psychic readings and psychometry.

From pretty normal lady who can just read people, through classic medium, to energy healer – psychics have many, many names. The best way to explain who psychic truly is, would be to say – psychics are highly intuitive people, which means they "know things" – they know about energies because they sense them, they know about you because they can read you, they know about the spirit because they can see it and so on.

It's important to understand that not every psychic is medium, but every medium is psychic. It means that not every psychic can talk to spirits and communicate with those who passed away. Some psychics have more gentle gifts like advanced intuition, and they can provide intuitive counselings and give psychic readings. Others are good in energy work and can utilize their skills as psychic healers. Some intuitive psychics can apply their abilities to work in the field of crime investigations or so called para-archeology and locate archaeological sites and support historical research. It's a good time to explain some common misconceptions about psychics.

Common Misconceptions About Psychics

Psychics do have different names, specializations, and opinions about themselves. And of course, different people perceive psychics differently. Before we move further, I want to discuss some common misconceptions regarding psychics, as the knowledge here might help you in the future, when you will have to explain others who you really are, and what is it that you do.

Crystal Ball And Such

One of the most popular misconceptions I have ever encountered in my psychic practice, is that people, when they hear the word 'psychic', think that this is an old lady sitting in a dark room illuminated by candles. And there's that dark table, on which there's the crystal ball. And of course, it is mandatory for such psychic to speak in mysterious tone, using weird words.

Well, of course this is true. In case of fake psychics, at least. I never encountered a real psychic that would agree with the short description in the last paragraph. In reality, all psychics that I know, looks pretty normal. They wear normal clothes (hey, I wear my t-shirt with AC/DC logo, proudly); they eat meat; they listen to music and so on. Honestly, most New Age fans have a greater tendency to look like a psychic than psychics themselves. This doesn't mean that no real psychic will look like from TV, of course. Some might prefer to look this way. But know this, most psychics look more normal than you think.

Every Psychic Gift Is The Same

Another common misconception is that every psychic gift is the same. There's a saying we have: "every medium is psychic, but not every psychic is a medium". Some people think that every psychic sees spirits, and can communicate with those who passed away. Well, it's not true. I can't see spirits, but I know people who can. On the other hand, they can't use a pendulum, while I have no problem with this. I know psychics who can do psychic readings, but are unable of perceiving astral bodies. And finally, I know psychics who can see auras, but they can't do psychic readings.

There are different psychic abilities, different skills to learn, different gifts to awake. And while it is possible to find two psychics who will be capable of doing the same thing, by using the same ability, it's funny, at least, to think that every psychic have the same set of skills - psychic tools. In reality, every psychic is different. And even more than this, let's think of an experiment. Place two psychics who can see auras in the same room, and ask them to describe your aura. You can be sure that they will describe it differently.

Now this requires an explanation, because it's one of the most popular arguments of skeptics, trying to prove that psychics are faking things. Skeptics think that "if two psychics doesn't get the same results, then it means that both of them are faking things". Honestly, it's a proof of ignorance of the skeptics in question, not legitimacy of psychics themselves. I have never, ever met another psychic who would be able to see the same things I see. Well, OK, maybe I did. There is that buddy of mine, we agree on one thing, that chakras looks not like vortexes, but like LED lights in the dark, that's all.

Reality is complex. Two psychics can perceive the same thing differently. It is because, when they are using their inner psychic senses, their perception is translated by their perception filters. Perception filters are their beliefs, knowledge, experiences etc. It's hard to describe the difference with mere words, so I will give you an example.

I was doing a chakra reading for a friend. Normally, every single guidebook to chakras says that 4th chakra, Heart, glows with color green. This was normal in my case; this is what I have learned, and this is what I have encoded in my memory as perception filter. And normally, I was perceiving green Heart chakra. Until the time of the reading in question, when I saw the chakra of my friend glowing orange.

"What the heck?!", I said. I didn't understand that at first, and about a month had passed before I learned what orange meant in that case. I did the following: I asked myself a simple control question "what does orange means to me", and my intuition gave me the answer. In my case, orange on the level of Heart chakra means "warm soul", or "warm heart". I think about it is as a sweet time spent with my grandma.

Somewhere, sometime during my life, orange was recorded in my subconscious mind as color, that represents positive, caring emotions towards others. How, why and when did it happened, I do not know, I can't find this in my memory. But it is there, and it shapes my psychic perception. It's my small psychic perception filter. Anyway, this is my own experience. But while I see that positive emotions of the person as orange Heart, another psychic sees normal, green color. Others can see shapes, and other objects, or even letters, hear sounds, and smell things. All of this in case of that one chakra. It's because, in different lives, the same emotions - positive, warm and caring - were recorded as psychic filters differently. To me, orange is warm, caring color. But someone else might smell grandma's cookies, and it will mean the same thing - love, warm and care.

By the way, whenever you will be doing psychic readings or aura readings and things like that, and you will perceive different colours, symbols, events and scenes, ask yourself that control question "what does ... means", and listen to your intuitive answer. It's a great way of learning what most of your psychic symbols means. By learning them, you will improve the accuracy of your psychic readings.

One more thing, notice that I have used bold font above, regarding the level of Heart chakra. Pay attention here, because as you will learn soon, orange is normally the color of the 2nd chakra, Sacral. But in this case, my perception is nearly the same as you will read in this book, and in other guidebooks to chakras. At the same time, in my own case, orange Heart has completely different meaning.

Different psychics perceive different colors, different symbols, different sounds and smells. And it's all within their psychic perception filters. And these filters are based on psychic's life, his or hers emotions, experiences, beliefs, knowledge, books the person read, opinions the person learned. So no, not every psychic is the same...

Psychic Abilities Are Gifts

Another false belief is that psychic abilities are gifts, and they cannot be learned. Well, if that would be the truth, then this entire book would be useless. But I'm living proof that psychic abilities can be learned from scratch. And I know other people who can say the same thing. So basically, don't believe that psychic abilities are gifts - sometimes they come as a gift, when some unexpected psychic ability awakes during your development. But everyone can become psychic with a bit of training.

Psychics Are Very Spiritual

This misconception results in beliefs that true psychic does not eat meat, have no sex, drinks only water, use beautiful, spiritual words spoken in very spiritual tone, drink no alcohol, listens only to New Age music and chants. Well, what I have just described applies – but not to psychics, rather to New Age believers, really. Or maybe I'm just wrong type of psychic. Personally, I'm really normal person. I drink coffee; I like beer; good wine; and a bottle of scotch. I eat meat, I like sex, I listen to AC/DC, Iron Maiden, Nightwish, and few heavy metal bands. I also like Trance music. I do, however, eat a lot of vegetables, mediate a lot, listen to Tibetan chants and drink water.

Being psychic is sometimes more about accepting yourself and embracing the fact that you're 100% human than becoming spiritual follower of New Age beliefs. These are good news for you. If you like heavy metal or meat, then listen and eat and enjoy the fact that you have been granted with a physical body that can enjoy physical pleasures. Enjoy your life! This is your first psychic development lesson!

Oh, and we are not free of ego, as well. But you must understand – true ego is your shield against the world. True ego is self-confidence minus being an asshole, as I used to say. Do not think that becoming a psychic will force you to get rid of your ego. Spiritual growth will, at some point, cause this to happen. But psychic development requires an ego. Because with ego, you know what you really want, you don't care about negative opinions of others, and you're not easily manipulated by people. You're self-confident in your abilities, and goals. Keep this in mind.

Psychics are very human. We're just people who are more intuitive than most of the population. But beside that, psychic is flesh and blood, with human needs, human flaws, but also – with human potential to become someone better.

You Are Psychic, No Matter of Your Age

Many people think that it takes many, many years to develop psychic abilities. Indeed, this is partially true – in order to master some abilities, you will spend many, many years learning and practicing. But to awake your psychic potential, the range varies from months, to one or two years. All you have to do is to practice few times a week, and the gates of the psychic world will be opened to you. And don't worry about your age, as well. You can be 15 years old, or 90 years old – you can still awake psychic abilities. Some people say that psychic development comes with age, but this isn't true – as I said, you can be a teenager with psychic abilities. Younger age is an advantage in the field of psychic development, really. The younger you are, the less number of blockages you have, and the faster your can learn.

Especially because of morphognetic fields, the theory created by Rupert Sheldrake, translated into raw "psychic" says: the more people learn something, the easier it is to learn that thing for others. In plain words, the more people in the world learn how to use computer, the easier it is for others to learn how to use computer. It's like the learning information is sent into the astral planes, and then "downloaded" by your mind when you're trying to learn something.

Because of this, the more people awakening their psychic potential means that more people can awake their psychic potential, and they can do this easier and faster. This also gives you additional advantage. When you know about morphogenetic fields, then you know, as well, that it's better to learn among other psychic practitioners, or in a place, where many people have awakened their psychic potential. But even if there's no such place or group of people near your place, don't worry. Through this book, you can still achieve your psychic goal.

How Psychic Do You Want To Become

The true question is not how to awake your psychic abilities, but how 'psychic' do you want to become? What skills do you want to learn, what abilities do you want to develop? What is your primary goal? Why do you want to become psychic? Do you want to use psychic abilities consciously, to give psychic readings, find missing people, see auras and energy fields? Or do you just want to start noticing psychic phenomena going on around you and you will be happy just by randomly experiencing things? On this decision, one thing depends - the length of your psychic development. The longer you will work with your psychic self, the greater control over your skills you will gain.

There are many different people who would like to start their psychic path. It will be sufficient to name the few:

- **Scientists** - Those, who would like to experience psychic phenomena, and research it under scientific conditions.
- **X-Man Wannabes** - kids and teenagers who would like to become superheroes.
- **Spiritual Explorers** - people tired by old religions, seeking illumination.
- **Psychics Themselves** - already psychics, who seeks ways of improving their "gifts".

- And of course normal people, who just know there's something more than the physical world.

No matter what type of person you are, sooner or later, if you will devote at least an hour per day for your psychic development, a lot of things will change. The ultimate need for proving the reality of psychic phenomena might be gone, replaced by the need of self-improvement. It's how "prove-it-all" skeptics change from skeptics into believers, who seek no desire to prove anything.

The magical wish of becoming superhero might be gone, replaced by a simple path of self-improvement. Personally, I was the person interested in becoming superhero - of course, it didn't work as I planned at first. But from the perspective of all these years, I regret nothing - thanks to my interest in developing psychic abilities, I became slightly more spiritually aware, and I've focused on improving myself. It doesn't mean I meditate for hours, I'm just trying to be a better person each day. Yes, I get angry from time to time, I get sad or tired, I'm normal human being, still. But a being, that is trying to change the way things are.

A Matter Of Intentions

You must be aware of your intentions. There are different intentions you might have. You might want to become psychic in order to help people. This is a good intention, and you should follow it. But you might also want to learn how to perform psychic healing only to use the skill to get in physical contact with young girls. This is a bad intention that might lead you to a bad place. You need to identify your true intentions first, before moving into psychic development.

Make a list of your psychic goals, answer the question: "why do I want to become psychic". And answer this question honestly. Be honest with yourself, it's one of the primary rules regarding inner growth. No one else will see these answers, because they're private. When you're done with the list, read it. Make sure that there are only positive intentions on it. It's OK to make money with psychic abilities, but it should not be your primary intention. Helping people, growing, learning – these are good things. But if there are bad intentions on your list, you need to deal with them first. That is one the first skills to learn will be meditation, affirmations and emotional healing.

> *Everyone has different goals. I wanted to become superhero at first. And I can't see anything bad here. But if you want to learn psychic powers in order to take revenge of some sort, then it's not the best idea.*
>
> *I know people who wanted to become psychics in order to improve their lives, just like that. They wanted to be better friends, better businessman, better teachers, better lawyers. Psychic potential, once unleashed, can be used in many different ways – not only for professional psychic readings, or psychic healing, but in simple daily issues, like taking care of your finances, or your family.*
>
> *If you want to improve your life without hurting anyone, and because of this you want to become psychic, then this is good intention. There's nothing wrong in improving your life. True psychic development will even persuade you to change your life for better.*
>
> *Teacher, businessman, chairman, policeman, ghost hunter, psychologist, lawyer, doctor; it doesn't matter*

> *who you are or who you want to become. In any field of human existence, psychic abilities will help you. As long as you want to improve your life, and hurt no one, then your intentions are OK. Of course, I encourage you to help others, and improve life of others, as well.*

Bad intentions can attract negative energies that might create problems in your life. But if you have bad intentions, don't worry about it right now. We will get to the point when you will work these out. For now, just take care of your list. Place it somewhere, so you won't loose it. You can already prepare yourself a psychic notebook, your journal of psychic development. I will discuss that thing a little bit further.

What Should You Learn, Really?

I need to point out one important thing, something that most people fail to realize. Let's be clear - people seek to develop psychic abilities through meditation, Yoga, mantras, Tai Chi Chuan, technology like Hemi Sync, even drugs of a different sort. People read over countless numbers of guidebooks and autobiographies of psychics, and when they find a suitable development method, they practice it for a while, and forget about it, beginning their journey once again. They think that the simplest methods of becoming psychic won't satisfy them, that they're not effective.

So a person jumps from a system to the system, and after many years, he or she have no psychic abilities at all. But, really? The truth is - and I have learned this after jumping from a system to system - the answers you seek, lies within. Within your mind, it's all there. All you need to do is to shut the hell up and start to listen. The psychic path is about listening. Read the book carefully and pay attention to the words. Remember - you're a Buddha. You have a potential to become a Buddha.

And you can achieve everything - and just like in case of any Buddha, your power is hidden in your mind. The term "Buddha" is... just a term. It describes every person in the world and the person's potential to become someone else, someone illuminated. There is an old story of three wise gods.

> *Three wise gods were discussing where should they hide the ultimate power. First of the gods said that they should hide it at the bottom of the ocean, yet the two other gods opposed as they were sure the man will finally find a way to the bottom of the ocean, and he will take the power. Second god said they should hide the power at the top of the tallest mountain, yet again, two other gods opposed. They were sure the man will find his way to the top, and he will take the power. Then the third, the oldest and wisest god said, "Let's hide the power within the man himself - he will never think of searching for it there" - the two other gods agreed. And thus, the true power lies within us, and we are not even aware of it.*

You don't need to be a Buddhist in order to believe in that power thing. But know this - answers to becoming psychic lies within your mind, all the exercises which you're about to learn, are simple meant to teach you how to work with your mind, and what to look for. Once again I have to say this – you are psychic already. But if you are, then why you're not aware of this?

Kids Are Psychics, Or – Why Are You An Unawakened Psychic

Kids are psychics – but not all of them. To understand this, you have to accept the possibility of reincarnation. Let me explain it to you now. Each life on Earth is meant for soul improvement. We're here to evolve on a spiritual level. Through different practices, soul that is immortal, can either evolve spiritually, or devolve, fall deeper into darkness. Spiritual practices like Buddhism pushes the soul's evolution further, while black magick, or ego magick practices causes the soul to devolve. All of this happens on the energetic level, and because of astral mechanics, the state of the soul and energy bodies is transferred from incarnation to incarnation. Soul is like a recording device. It records your Karma: your good and bad deeds. After dead, the soul goes to the Source (God, Absolute, Universe, whatever you call it), and then it goes back to the material world to incarnate again.

After being reborn in the material world, it takes some time, months or years, before etheric bodies will develop to a significant level. During that time, all kids are connected to the Source, and they can draw energies from the Source (a reason why kids are so creative, peaceful and happy, and why they grow so fast). During the etheric bodies development, two things might happen. First, Karma might happen – and the memory of the soul will recreate blockages on etheric bodies, causing the chakras and energy channels (Meridians) to be blocked, thus shutting down psychic abilities, and blocking psychic potential.

If Karma won't happen, then the society will, especially in the Western World. Our modern Western civilization is based on logic, rational thinking and materialistic instincts, chasing money and career. Telling kids that they should shut up; blocking their creativity in school; screaming at them; biting them; teaching them that life is difficult; that money are the most important thing in the world; that true love doesn't exist; that they should care only about themselves; that humanity is dangerous and so on... All of this creates blockages on the etheric bodies, thus causing psychic abilities to shut down.

Actually, there is a third thing that might happen – child might be born with chakras so nicely opened, and with so little negative Karma, that the society won't be able to block the kid entirely, and psychic abilities will become an important part of the kid's life. That's how born psychics are... "born" - they're simple not blocked by the society or their previous lives. And through exploration of psychic phenomena and spiritual growth, they can only improve their abilities further and further.

This is how things look like – but you don't have to believe in reincarnation in order to achieve psychic awakening. All you need to accept is the fact that there are blockages on your etheric bodies that need to be removed. Why so? The fact is, in order to become psychic and use Extra-Sensory Perception, Intuition and to improve your sensitivity to psychic energies. You need to open your chakras and clear energy channels. When they're dirty, filled with negative energies, the pure life energy – Chi – is unable to undisturbed flow. Because of this, not only you can experience physical or emotional problems, like illnesses or depression, but your chakras won't receive enough energy. Thus, they won't be able to "plug" into the energies flowing around you, containing useful information, and they won't be able to attune to intuitive thinking and so on. Chakras development is important for every psychic wannabe.

You can say that awakening psychic abilities is all about clearing the mess in your mind and in your chakras. And this is what I teach – how to deal with the mess.

But what kind of blockages are we talking about, actually? Generally, a blockage is a negative emotion. For example, when you're angry, you might create blockage. If you're scared, it can be another blockage, when you suffer from emotional trauma, it's a blockage, definitely. How are blockages created? It's simple - negative patterns (like intolerance towards religion) and negative emotions, changes the vibrations of the energies in your body, and because of this, these energies are simple stuck, either in chakras or in the energy channels - and they root, like old meat.

Any negative emotion like anger, fear or trauma can create blockage. Any negative pattern that is related to negative emotions (negative thinking, intolerance, hate) can create blockages. And there's no place for negative emotions and patterns in psychic's mind.

That's why you might be an unawakened psychic. You might have too many blockages that make it impossible for you to connect with your intuition. It's that simple.

Psychic Development Is About Mind And Energy Work

Psychic awakening is about working with your mind – through meditation, affirmations and emotional healing, in order to remove subconscious blockages, that results in energy blockages. It's also about energy work, collecting more life energy (Chi, psychic energy), recognizing the blockages, and learning how to manipulate energies through your Will in order to acquire information, or to affect other energies (for example for the purpose of energy healing). This book focuses on these things – soon you will learn how energy work and breathing can help you identify blockages, how affirmations and meditation can remove these blockages, and how you can develop your abilities further.

That's it – it's very simple in theory, very simple in practice, and the only difficulty you might face is your patience.

Patience is important – you shouldn't expect fast results. I can say more, don't expect any results at all, just focus on working with your mind and energies as this Course says. Results will come sooner or later, when you will be ready, but don't think about them. Think about practicing, not about the result, as it might block you. Thinking of your ultimate, final goal can block your perception to such degree, that you won't notice your sensitivity improved; your intuition be louder; your natural psychic gifts awaken. Through the exercises from this book and meditation, you will learn patience as a side effect, if I may say that.

You also need to know that there are no guidelines set for the speed of your development. One of the most important things for you to know is that the skills you're about to learn will develop faster or slower and that the speed depends on many things. For example, your diet, depending on what you eat specific nutrient might affect the speed of psychic development; also, physical exercises like swimming or running might take an important part here. I have said earlier that, usually, psychic awakening takes from few months to about two years. Of course, this isn't a general rule – in your case, it might take more or less time.

Also, remember that everyone is different, for some people use of psychic abilities is very natural, they're born this way, for others, it's a skill like any other, and they have to learn it from scratch. For some people, the learning process takes weeks, for others it may take years. There are no set guidelines for this, and you must consider the fact that you might be the person that will require years of practice before noticing any results. What I understand is that each person in the world is a 'PSI-positive' and by this, is capable of developing psychic skills to some level.

Therefore, do not worry if you won't notice any results after few weeks or months of practice, just remain patient, it might take some time. And what matters the most, do not worry after not getting any result at first or second trial. Practice is the key when it comes to developing psychic abilities. Also, keep in mind that there blockages are constantly being created. They can block your entire development. For example, if you will focus on not getting any results, your thoughts, charged with emotions, will be recorded into memory. Memory is the negative thought pattern, and it can kick in any time, when you will expect results. In the end, your subconscious itself will block your results, and you won't make any progress. Therefore, your second real lesson of psychic development is simple – do not expect any results. Practice, and do not worry about anything else. Just observe, and at some point, you will notice the progress you want. But do not expect it.

Know this – psychic development is like tuning in into a source of infinitive information, creativity and inspiration. Imagine that psychic energies that are transferring information and inspiration like radio waves, are being emitted by a radio tower in all directions, and the range of these waves is unlimited; therefore, you're in the range, too. You are being affected by the waves, but you can't really pick them up, while some people can. These who can are just tuned-in to right frequencies, all you have to do is to tune-in yourself to the right frequency just like "gifted" people do. This tuning-in process might take months or years... Or sometimes just weeks. But it's possible to achieve by everyone.

For now, let's discuss something more practical.

First Step in Working Out Your Blockages

I've mentioned psychic blockages in few places already, and it's time to explain how to deal with these blockages – of course, it will be just first step. In order to start removing your blockages, you need to start learning the theory of psychic phenomena. Why do you need theory? Let's skip the obvious reason that goes like this: you need to know how things work, in order to use psychic skills, period. Theory expands your awareness. Because of the blockages you might have, especially these that have taught you to dump your creativity, or not to trust your intuition and focus on rational thinking, your subconscious mind will simple deny the fact that you can become psychic. And you might think consciously that your subconscious mind is wrong, but hey – it's your subconscious mind, it governs your entire body and most of your thinking. You can't just say it that it's wrong. No, you need to redefine your thinking.

Reading about psychic phenomena is the first step toward psychic awakening. Your subconscious mind, through reading books, articles and theoretical ideas, begins to think that psychic abilities might be actually possible. Your sub-c begins to acknowledge that there are many possibilities of utilizing your psychic abilities by reading about different psychic abilities. For this reason, I always recommend reading a lot of books about psychic abilities and psychic experiences. And this will be your first homework.

Visit your local library, and grab as many books about psychic phenomena as possible. And start reading, just like that. If you can't find any books in your library, try local bookstore – you don't need to buy anything, just sit there and read. Building up your psychic library is also a great idea, because it creates an element of 'hobby', I may say. Beside the fact, in case of many people, collecting things is enjoyable, building your own psychic library might benefit in the future. For example, when you will require some additional references in your psychic work, whether you will be professional psychic, or not, such library might come in handy.

Finally, there's Internet. Beside reading articles on my website, A State of Mind, there are countless websites out there, which you can read. Of course, reading this book is also a way to do this homework.

Are You Psychic Already?

Of course, words are not enough - if everyone is capable of using psychic abilities, so can you, right? And you want to proofs for that right now, and that's perfectly understandable. So now I'm going to give you some practical proofs that you can really manipulate psychic energies, and use psychic abilities.

Let's try with something simple at first, please take few minutes and answer the following questions.

- Have you ever felt the phone is about to ring? If so, then you had a premonition, a simple sign of innate psychic abilities. Of course, it might have been simple coincidence, but if you can count more than two such situations, then there's something going on.
- Have you ever had a dream that came true? If yes, then know it was a precognitive dream, and you have dreamed about the future – it's a psychic thing. I can recall dreaming about many things that came true. Can you?
- Have you ever entered a room and you felt something? Have you knew people were gossiping about you? Therefore, you have picked up information flowing along with psychic energies of this room - so called psychic-impressions.
- Have you ever sensed someone staring at you behind your back? Then you have sensed psychic energies carrying specific psychic impressions, something many people never pay attention to.
- Have you ever sensed any presence in a haunted home? If so, then heck – you have felt psychic signature, the very energy body of the entity haunting the place. Of course, only if you ever been in haunted place.
- Have you ever felt growing levels of energy in sunny morning, or during a sunset? Then you have felt the beauty of psychic energies that flow all around the

world, and different frequencies of the different part of the day.

Such things - knowing that something is about to happen, intuitive thoughts, sensing weird things, having weird dreams, that's what I call a passive proofs for psychic phenomena. Yet the above might not be enough for you, and you want some real energy work, right? Great, you're interested! OK, let's get to work - here are some practical exercises.

Let me give you a simple energy work exercise. Focus on your big thumb in your dominant hand. Touch it with your index finger of your other hand and start "drawing" circles. While doing this, focus on the sensation of touch, focus on the circles you physically feel. After a minute, take your index finger away, but keep feeling the touch – imagine the touch and focus on it (close your eyes if you prefer). Do this for few minutes. What do you feel? Warm, cold, tingling, pressure, anything weird or extraordinary? Yep, what you feel is psychic energy making circles in this little part of your energy system. And that's tactile visualization, something you're going to work with for the next few months.

Or let's try to make a very basic psiball and see how good you are.

Imagine you're holding a ball, move your hands into physical position. Visualize, or in other words, imagine the energy coming from Earth through your legs and torso, to your hands and palms, then to a space between your palms and forming a shape of a ball. You can visualize the energy as bright light - that should be enough. Keep visualizing the energy moving from Earth to that space and visualize you're making a ball. After few minutes, stop and focus on the ball you have created – what do you feel? If you sense something at all, then congratulations – you just created a psiball. If you want more, here its.

Or, let's warm up your hands. Clap your hands three times, then put your both palms together, and start rubbing them for about 30 seconds. After that, hold your palms facing each other, with about 1-2 inches of space between them. Try to increase and decrease the distance between your palms, what do you feel? If it's pressure, then you have just warmed up your hands, and you can sense psychic energies between your palms.

Persuaded? And that's just the beginning of your psychic work. But don't worry if you did not sense anything. Some people are really blocked, and they might not be able to know things, or sense psychic energies. This might mean that you will have to spend more time working with your mind, but in the end, you will get results.

A Matter of Gift

Psychic abilities are skills that you can learn. But you have heard about psychic 'gifts', as well. This is one of the common psychic misconceptions, which I spoke about. But let's repeat the question: are psychic abilities gifts, or skills? I would say – both. As psychic practitioner, you can learn everything. But sometimes, some abilities might just awake on their own, during your psychic development. Like one day, you might figure out that you can do something psychically, something I haven't talked about, and maybe even something that has never been described in any of the sources. In such case, I say – go for it! And explore the new gift you received.

How is it that some abilities just awake? My theory is simple: I believe that some people have a potential to use specific abilities, but the potential is hidden and it requires psychic development to awake. It's like everyone have that one or two psychic 'gifts', and a whole potential to learn more than that. But if he or she will begin to work with mind and psychic energies, some natural abilities will just awake, and they will be there, no matter if you want to develop further, or not.

Preparing Your Notebook

Because psychic development is about working with both mind and energies, there is a strong need to have something physical we could focus on. Without such a thing, we can easily get distract and bore by practicing psychic abilities. Focus can be achieved by using specific physical objects that will support you in reaching your goals. One of such 'physical' elements is collecting books about psychic development.

But also, during your psychic awakening, you should keep a journal. Months ago, I had nothing against managing your journal on a computer, but today, I only advise keeping a paper journal. The reason behind this is simple. By writing something on paper, you're using more parts of your brain and it's yet another technique of working with your subconscious. The more brain power is devoted to writing down about your psychic experiences and psychic progress, the more persuaded your subconscious becomes. It's like reprogramming your mind to believe that psychic phenomena is real.

Use your journal to write notes of your psychic growth. Write down your psychic experiences (for example, knowing things, or sensing people and energies), feelings and sensations during psychic exercises, and your thoughts about psychic abilities and your psychic potential. Write down your intuitive thoughts, and results of psychic readings and psychometry, when you will get to that point. Make your journal your best friend during your psychic awakening.

When you will get to the point of inner psychic sight, and psychic readings, write down the meanings of symbols and colors you will perceive during your practice.

ot asking you to consider having a journal, really – you
know, it's mandatory. So go to a local store or purchase
notebook online. Personally I always suggest Moleskines, as
they are fine notebooks, but you need to enjoy your notebook, so
if you don't like Moleskines, choose any type of notebook.
Enjoy your journal. Write in it, draw, paint, have fun. It's
another way of programming your subconscious mind.

Make a note in your journal

Make the first note in your journal – mark the date (you will mark dates on all future notes, OK?). Write down who you are, what you want to learn, what do you expect, what things you already know, and what skills you already have (if any). Just write it down, and then continue reading. Attach the list with your intentions and goals, which you have prepared earlier.

Beside books and notebooks, you might want to create a passion board, as well. It's a corkboard that you can hang on the wall. On it, you can put photos and notes (and other different things) related to psychic phenomena, things that will help you focus on your goals. Each day you will see the board in front of you, and, by doing so, you will remind yourself what you are about to learn. It's like scrap-booking – it's fun, and it programs your subconscious. Again.

The Importance Of Practice Partner

Many books that discuss psychic development mention that it is crucial to have a practice partner, a person to test psychic abilities with. I admit that more advanced techniques cannot be learned alone and practice partner is required, indeed. For example, in energy sending and receiving, psychometry, psychic readings, or telepathy it's nearly impossible to learn and develop new skills if you're alone. But basic arts like energy manipulation, opening chakras, creating psiballs or even energy pulsing and sensing - these skills can be learned on your own and no practice partner is needed.

For some exercises that require practice partner, I will be also describing how to perform that exercises alone. This can be considered as cold practice when you can learn half of the ability alone. Yet, if you have a possibility to practice with another person, do this. How to find practice partner? Look among your friends and family, maybe someone will be interested? Personally, I've found a great practice partner in my girlfriend when she turned out to be a great potential energy worker.

What is interesting is the fact, that once you will start meditating, working with affirmations and healing your emotions, and working with energies, you will notice that thanks to your intuition, your ESP abilities are developing any way. So don't worry, really, if you don't have practice partner yet. For now, just focus on your own, individual growth.

Short History Of Psychic Development

Psychic abilities had been in use for thousands of years. Even when we skip the theoretical existence of Atlantis, we still have a lot to talk about. For many hundreds of years, psychic abilities that were perceived as magick, had been present in ancient Egypt within priest caste. Ancient Greeks had so called oracles - the most famous one was located in Delphi. During Dark Ages, healers of a different sort were psychics (if they weren't frauds). Psychics were living in India and China, too. Those countries created a huge amount of texts related to psychic energies. From texts about Chakras, to texts about martial art of Tai Chi Chuan.

For thousands of years, and for this very day, tribal shamans are psychics too. During the period between Middle Ages and Industrial Revolution mages and occultists were considered those with psychic abilities. For many years, before the time of steam and technology, people with psychic abilities were hiding, and those who were developing these skills were learning them in secret.

In Eastern world, psychics abilities were taught by a master to student. And in other places of the world, shamans were being chosen by spirits themselves, and it was impossible for a tribe member to become a shaman just because he wanted to - it was up to the spirits.

And the Victorian Age came to be, people become more interested in learning about psychic abilities from a practical perspective. Organizations like Society for Psychical Research were founded, and their goal were to study the mysterious phenomena of psychic abilities.

And with the second half of XX century, conscious psychic development become a field of interest, first by governments of United States and Soviet Union, then of civilian parties. Groups of psychic practitioners were forming, and with the age of Internet revolution, now everyone can find resources about ways to develop psychic abilities.

I recognize that it is very, very short history of psychic development, but it proves the point – the fact that psychic abilities are part of the entire mankind since we have left caves. It's very natural to have psychic abilities. Today, people like you are making history. Just by learning things that are labeled "impossible" by many.

Summary

You have learned that you're already psychic, but you might be blocked. And you have learned two steps towards psychic awakening – reading psychic-related books, and realizing the fact that you are psychic already. For now, you have your homework: reading psychic-related materials: books, articles and websites. Relax now, and enjoy the fact that you've made two steps forward already. Relax, because you know you're psychic – learning how to use your abilities is just a matter of time and practice.

The Essence Of Theory

"Knowledge Talks, Wisdom Listens"

Theory comes first, because you should understand what role the energies play in psychic phenomena and your entire psychic potential, how to collect them, and how they influence your life. Pay attention during this lesson, as you will learn useful information how to make sure you always have a high level of energies.

Psychic Energies

Psychic abilities require fuel to work, in at least two ways. First of all, energy is required to charge chakras and every single cell of our body. Every cell requires life energy, Chi. It's Chinese term, and you might be familiar with other terms as well, for example, Prana, Qi, Orgone, Odic Force, Mana. Second of all, in many psychic abilities, for example, psychic readings, energies work like active sonar, you first send energies to collect information, and then these energies are returning to you, so you need to have enough energy to send them away. And in psychic healing, you're also using your own energies by transferring them to ill body.

You need energies to develop your chakras, and use your psychic abilities later; therefore, you should learn how to take care of your energies.

Chi can be divided into two – imagine that you have fuel canister divided into two sections. In the first section, there is normal Chi, that is constantly being used and recharged. In the second section, you have born Chi, the energy that has been given to you by your parents in the day you were conceived. This energy defines the length of your life, actually, and when this energy is gone, the body dies. This energy cannot be recharged.

For this reason, it is unwise to use psychic abilities after your normal Chi reserves are depleted. What can deplete your Chi?

- **Using psychic abilities, of course** – it's obvious, the more psychic abilities you're using, the more energy you spent.
- **Living** – each day of your life requires energies. This includes negative emotions like anger or fear, and of course stress.

- **Sex** – in case of males, sex depletes your energies, as you're sending them to female's body, so it can fill the fetus later on. That's why if you're a male, you should either learn how to control your sexual energies, limit your sexual activities, or focus on providing your body with more energies than an average person. Ladies have an advantage here. They actually collect more energies during sex.
- **Drugs, smoking, alcohol, tea and coffee,** these substances are destroying your organism. Some are stronger or weaker than others. It's a good idea to stop drinking alcohol, tea and coffee (I'm not mentioning drugs, it's obvious that you shouldn't use them), or at least limit it. I drink all these things, yet I'm still psychic – but I'm trying to limit the amount of all these drinks.
- **Fast food and microwave food** - fast food is filled with toxins, and microwave food is simple deprived of life energies. Do not eat fast foods, or foods prepared in microwave.
- **Energy drinks** – these treacherous drinks do only one thing, they push your organism to its limits, draining your Chi like psychic vampire. Don't use energy drinks at all.
- **Negative thoughts and patterns** – hate, jealousy, intolerance, aggression and other negative mind patterns, all of this can also deplete your energies.

Now, when you know these things, you know what should you do to limit the amount of energies you're wasting. Limit the amount of alcohol, tea and coffee that you drink, drop totally fast foods, microwave foods and energy drinks. Don't worry, by happy – seriously, relax and limit your stress and negative emotions. That last part can be difficult, as our emotions are often governed by our habits. With time and effort, thanks to affirmations and emotional healing, you will notice that you're more peaceful, and that negative emotions are slowly disappearing.

To give you better example of the amount of your drinks, here's what I drink – one beer each two weeks, one coffee per day, two cups of tea pear day, and once a month, I enjoy small glass of scotch. And I still have enough energy to work with my chakras, and use my psychic abilities. It would be even better to stop drinking alcohol, tea and coffee totally, but let's not go that far. I will say this – it's OK to enjoy beer and coffee. With your progress, at some point you might sense that it is time to drop coffee, and you will do this, with no objections or problems. The same thing might happen with tea and alcohol, at some point through your developing intuition, you might just feel that it is time to change your diet again. And when you feel it's time for change – follow your intuition, just like that. But if you enjoy a cup of coffee once a day, then just keep enjoying it.

Changing your habits based on the knowledge above, you will make another step towards your psychic awakening. It would be a good idea, as well, to stop watching movies in which there's a lot of killing, or stop listening to dark, evil music. Negative words, sounds and scenes create low-vibration energies, and this is not good for your psychic growth.

You should also start eating healthy food, especially when you prefer junk food so far. Common suggestion that can be found within many different psychic development sources is that you should switch yourself to a vegetarian diet, if you ever want to become psychic at all. Although I say that you should switch to a healthy diet, saying that vegetarianism is mandatory is not true, at least not in 100%. It is just a misconception and lack of knowledge regarding the purpose of fruits and vegetables in our diet. This is the rule you should apply in your diet, 80/20. Which means: 80% of vegetables and/or fruits, and 20% of meat.

Of course, this doesn't mean that you should limit the amount of meat you're eating. On the contrary, you can eat as much meat as you like. But you should not limit yourself to eating meat only, vegetables and fruits are also very important, not only because they contain a lot of vitamins and nutrients, but because they store high quantities of Chi within them. Eating high amount of fruits and vegetables is a way of increasing the amount of Chi flowing within your own body.

Rising Vibrations

You should also start rising the vibrations of your energy body. Vibrations are like frequency, that defines if the energy are positive or negative. The higher the vibrations of your energy body are, the better quality of energy flowing through you is. Because of this, I have another homework for you. From now on each morning, and each evening, say to yourself the following "prayer".

> *Just for today, be at peace,*
> *Just for today, be happy,*
> *Be kind to people,*
> *Focus on your work,*
> *And be thankful.*

These are the rules of a good life of Reiki, created by Mikao Usui in the early XX century. Allow me to explain them: When you're at peace, you're not depleting your energies – so don't worry. When you're happy, you're increasing the vibrations of your energies, turning them from negative or neutral, into positive, slightly more spiritual energies. So smile and be happy. When you're kind to people, you project positive energies, and because of the law of attraction, at the same time you're attracting positive energies. Devoting yourself to your work means that whatever you do, you should do with passion. And when you're thankful, once again you're projecting and attracting positive energies.

These are simple things – but they will start to change your own approach to life, changing the way you live, simple by opening you towards spiritual powers, and important things like friendship or honesty. They attract high-vibrational energies, which are simple healing you emotionally and spiritually, even if you're not aware of this. And it's another step towards psychic awakening. From now on, make sure that this short prayer becomes your habit each morning and each evening.

How To Recharge Your Batteries

Let's get back to psychic energies. Learning what depletes your energies is just one thing – you also need to know how to recharge your psychic batteries, so you can increase the amount of energies you have. This can be done through spending some time close to nature, or eating food filled with energies. You already know that fast food and microwave food depletes your energies. So what kind of food charge you with energies?

That will be fruits and vegetables – for this reason, vegetarianism is often associated with psychic development. As I said already, vegetarianism isn't mandatory. It's like with tea and coffee – if you will feel that you should switch entirely to vegetarianism, to do. But if you don't want to, and you enjoy eating meat, then continue eating meat. I know many psychics who are very advanced in their psychic journey, yet still enjoy eating meat.

But it doesn't change the fact, that your diet should be full of fruits and vegetables, especially fresh. They contain a lot of life energies that are later on acquired by your organism during the

...ss. Simple – less meat, more fresh vegetables and ...uits. Everything else depends on your personal feelings and intuition. But there's one more thing you should learn – that you need to learn how to eat your food.

Most people eat fast and with mind wondering. This is wrong, as this not only generates problems with physical digestion process, it also generates problems with the amount of energies you're collecting from food. So how to eat?

Food should be eaten slowly, and you should be focused on the process. You need to taste your food, and enjoy each and every bite. Also, before beginning to eat, say a prayer:

> *I, YOUR NAME, am thankful for this food I'm about to consume, I'm thankful to everyone thanks to whom I can enjoy this dish today.*

You must consider each of your dishes as spiritual experience. Threat your food with respect and enjoy it, just like that. This will make sure that a large amount of life energy will be collected by your energy body. Changing the way you eat is your another step towards psychic awakening.

Nature's Call

Food isn't the only way you can use to recharge your psychic batteries. As I said, you can also spend some time close to nature. Go for a walk to forest, or city park. Sit for a while on the ocean shore, or mountain stream, hug a tree. As human beings, we are part of Mother Nature, and we need direct contact to it, if we want to collect life energies. Nearly everyone have access to nature – it doesn't have to be wild rain forest, as I said, you can use small city park, or a tree in your backyard. It always is something.

Just by jogging in city park, or taking a walk, or spending 15 minutes near mountain creek, you can recharge yourself, it's easy step towards psychic awakening.

Of course, using nature's energies can be improved through energy work techniques, but I will teach you about this in another lesson. For now, here's your another homework. Spend at least 15 minutes each day close to nature. It's the preferable amount of time, but if you can't achieve this, then three times a week will be enough. From now on, try to spend as much time outside city life as possible, at least in city park near the trees.

The point of this is simple – to obtain more psychic energies to fuel your body, and your psychic abilities. This leads me to a subject of energy work, at last. Energy work, at least one that truly interests you now, is made of the following elements:

First, energy work is meant to draw additional psychic energies (Chi, Prana) into your body, both physical, and etherical, by using your conscious will. This improves your conscious control over life energies, and, in addition improves the overall amount, of the energies within your body.

Second, conscious energy work helps you cleanse your energy channels, and this allows more energy to flow into your chakras. Additional energy sometimes remove blockages, and sometimes it just "activates" them, so you have to deal with them using other methods, such as affirmations or emotional healing.

Part of this book is to teach you how to use one of the simplest energy work techniques currently in existence. I'm talking here about New Energy Ways, designed by Robert Bruce, mystic and author of numerous books, which I certainly recommend. But even if this system has been described in this book, there are many more energy work systems in the world. If you have access to, I recommend signing up for Yoga workshops. Yoga is meant to improve your physical body, and by doing so, to improve your energetics. Better than Yoga, in my opinion, is the art of Tai Chi Chuan. If you can, learn at least the basic 24 forms, and practice them few times a week in a forest, city park or ocean's shore. Tai Chi Chuan is meant not only to improve your body, but also to teach you how to improve your breathe, and how to draw additional life energies from your surrounding area.

> *You should know that you don't have to attend any workshop in order to study the basic 24 forms of Tai Chi Chuan. You can purchase a video course, but you can also find instructional videos for free on the Internet. Although I have to say two things.*
>
> *First, it always is a excellent idea to have a teacher, especially because Tai Chi Chuan is an art of working with psychic energies. But you can learn 24 forms from the Internet, knowing that, because it's energy work, your practice might lead to re-emerging of negative thought patterns, and emotional problems. But you already know ways to deal with these problems - affirmations and emotional healing, as well as meditation practice. All right, at least you know such methods exists, and that you will learn them step-by-step in few next chapters. Practicing Tai Chi Chuan in its basic form shouldn't be a problem for you, and it will make a fine addition to your psychic development practice.*
>
> *Second, many online tutorials tell you about Chi Kung (or Qi Gong), as well. You need to be aware of one thing. While Tai Chi Chuan works with Earth energies, living Chi, on the other hand, Chi Kung works with*

cosmic energies, more spiritual powers. Mixing these two types of energies at the same time isn't the best thing you can do. I always recommend that you wait at least one hour before Chi Kung practice, and Tai Chi Chuan practice, and vice versa.

I never practiced Yoga, really, but I have heard stories of people who weren't able to deal with the problems that resurfaced during their practice. Therefore, I can only speculate that you will be able to work out your problems with affirmations and emotional healing. Because of this, I strongly recommend that you should practice Yoga along with an experienced teacher, who perceive Yoga as something more, than just physical exercises.

If you're unable to learn Yoga nor Tai Chi Chuan at the moment, then New Energy Ways will be a great addition to your daily psychic development practice. But you have to be patient, New Energy Ways will be discussed later. For now, you need to learn, actually, what are you going to fuel. It's time to learn about your energy bodies and your chakras.

The knowledge about energy bodies has been brought to our attention thanks to Theosophical Society. But almost every psychic capable of perceiving energy bodies can confirm that Theosophical knowledge, based on Hindu teachings, is quite correct in this matter.

Energy Bodies

Now when you have learned a bit about life energies, it is time to learn about your etheric bodies. Energy bodies are part of the energy system – we say we have energy bodies, in which we have chakras and energy channels called "Meridians" (Chinese term) or Nadi (Hindu term).

Beside physical body, you also have etheric bodies, made of pure psychic energy. These bodies can be perceived through inner psychic sight, and soon I will teach you how to do this. But for now, you need to learn theory. There are three etheric bodies that interest you.

Etheric Body, also know as energetic body is the closest etheric body to the physical realm. It is the first body, in which you can see chakras and energy channels. It collects life energies and spends life energies to fuel physical cells. Blockages in this body can generate physical illnesses.

Second is Astral Body, and it's the body directly connected to our subconscious mind. Blockages in this body can be also perceived on the etheric body. It is Astral body where emotional blockages are created, through our subconscious blockages. When the blockage on the Astral body is removed, it is also removed on the etheric body, thus allowing life energies to flow freely.

Finally, there's Mental Body that stores ideals, thoughts and intuition.

Spiritual psychic energies like intuition go from higher body into the lower body – it means that your intuitive thoughts are flowing through Mental Body, then Astral Body, Etheric Body and when there are no blockages on their way, they reach physical body, and your brain, so you can acquire psychic information. That's why removing subconscious (and energetic) blockages is a step to psychic awakening and psychic development.

Energies that flow freely through energy bodies and reaches chakras - our energy exchange centers.

Chakras

Chakras exists in each and every energetic body – etheric, astral and mental. They are energy exchange centers, through which energies flow. Chakras can utilize energies to fulfill our desires, use psychic abilities, self-heal and so on. When they are blocked, the energy cannot be redirected to a specific task. For example, if the root chakra is blocked, you might be afraid of the material world, and if the third eye is blocked, you might be blocked from your psychic abilities. Therefore, understanding which chakra is responsible for which part of your life is an important step in your psychic awakening.

Some people say that chakras looks like funnels – I wouldn't say so. Chakras looks more like glowing balls of light, and their structure is quite simple – chakras are regions, when a high number of energy channels cross each other, creating density of energy channels, thus an area of high concentration of energy. Chakra is a term that comes from Hindu, and it means "Vortex" - in Hindu chakras science, chakras were always pictured with a specific number of petals – these petals are symbolic representations of a number of energy channels that cross each other in that specific area of the energy body. Anyway, this is just theoretical knowledge.

I'm mentioning it to teach you one thing – chakras are areas of high concentration of psychic energies (life energy, Chi), and that's all you should really keep in mind. Also, when you will learn how to perceive them, don't worry if they won't look like funnels or vortexes – personally, I see them look more like glowing LED in a dark room, really. Your perception, your inner sight, is subjective – it's based on your experience, knowledge and imagination. I see chakras as LED light, but you might see painted flower. And that's something you should keep in mind, always – your psychic perception is subjective.

Illustration 1: 7 chakras

Once you will understand chakras, it will be much easier to identify your emotional blockages that it is without chakras understanding. So, you will be able to remove the blockages not only through mind work (like affirmations, or emotional healing), but also through intensive energy work. Also, it will be helpful when you will learn how to scan chakras, to give basic psychic reading. Thus, you're going to learn about chakras now.

Usually, we're describing chakras from the bottom one to the top one – it's not mandatory, it's just simpler.

There are seven primary chakras – and thousands of smaller chakras. These smaller chakras shouldn't interest you until you decide for psychic healing practice, but since it's not the subject of this Course, I will not discuss them here. Anyway, ready? Let's we start with the first chakra.

1st Chakra – Root - Maladhara

This chakra is located between your anus and genitals. It is called Root, for two reasons: first, it's the first chakra (obviously), and second, because it often serve as grounding anchor, and a place, through which Earth energies flow into the energy system. It's like a root of a tree. It's a chakra of basic instincts that say "to eat, to copulate, to survive", and it's very materialistic, physical chakra. It's standard color is red.

Root chakra represents physical will to live, to survive. It's directly connected to the physical world, and Earth as Mother Nature – through this chakra, we sense we're part of the world we live in, and that we're part of nature. It's connected to our basic needs and things required to survive – for example, food. But also, in this materialistic modern world, things like money, house to live in, bed to sleep on. Beside such individual things, it's also connected to more "global" needs, like the need of global safety (like being safe from terrorism or famine).

This chakra helps you ground yourself, feel safe in the material world. When this chakra is harmonious, you feel safe, and you have the base to build your life upon. It's also a chakra connected to your human need to reproduce, to make sure our species survive.

Harmonious Work

When your chakra's work is harmonious, you feel that you're connected with Earth, that you're part of Mother Nature, that you're grounded and safe in this world. You feel that you have everything you need, and you trust the world to provide you with everything you need.

Disharmonious Work

But when your chakra's work is disharmonious, you're obsessed with the material world – you chase money and material goods, and material pleasures at the cost of spiritual wisdom. You don't feel safe, because you don't feel you have everything you need, there always is something you want, yet you cannot get. At the same time, you have problems with giving, or accepting gifts; you do not live in the present; and when you achieve your goals, you don't notice that, because there are still other things you need to achieve.

You might have problems with your diet, and you might forget about the needs of others – truly, you might be blind for the needs of others. You lack peace. And if you can't get what you want, you become aggressive, and you start to perceive people around you as your enemies. In the end, you fail to trust world around you, and you lose trust in people.

Blockages

When your Root chakra is blocked you might experience physical and mental weakness; you might suffer from both physical and mental illnesses. You're constantly afraid of the future, and you fail to enjoy the present. Instead of being happy with your life, you're paying attention to all your problems, and things that might be.

2nd Chakra – Sacral - Svadhisthana

The second chakra is located below your navel. Its standard color is orange, and it's often associated with sexuality. But that's just part of this chakra meaning. I would say it's related to reproduction and multiplication – but not only in sexual meaning, but also regarding multiplication of spiritual knowledge, or even physical goods that serve the mankind.

The second chakra is the source of primeval emotions – creativity, life force, sexuality. "I eat, I copulate, I survive", you might say, but it's very basic way to put it. It represents our sexuality, but in more esoteric meaning – think of it like a center for Yin and Yang energies, universal energies of creation. Through these energies, through the universal law of creation, we create new life, new ideas, new technologies, new thoughts and so on.

In regards of sexuality again, your second chakra is responsible for all kinds of relationship – boss to worker, friend to friend, mother to child, and of course – boy to girl, and girl to boy :). It also governs all erotic games, and sexual interaction.

This chakra also helps in our psychic cleansing process, helping us deal with stagnant emotions that are no longer needed – remove them, and you can experience life anew each day.

Harmonious Work

Harmonious work shows in your behaviour – you're open and natural towards other people, and opposite gender, you don't play games, you are just yourself. Your life is full of positive emotions that make you enjoy the beauty of the world around you each and every day. You're creative, and you enjoy the art of creation.

Disharmonious Work

You might experience lack of physical contact, which might generate emotional pain. You might want to negate your sexuality, and you might want to block your entire creativity. In result, you might experience too many sexual fantasies, and at the same time, you might be unable to creative thinking. You might feel aggression towards opposite gender, as well. All of this might lead to such kind of relationship, in which sex is most important, and love do not exist.

Blockages

Your creativity and sexuality is blocked, and you lack physical contact. This can results in being afraid of physical contact, touch, sex, or just the opposite gender. You might lack self-confidence, and emotional stagnation. And finally – you don't enjoy life.

3rd Chakra – Solar Plexux – Manipura

The third chakra's standard color is yellow, and it's primary related to shaping your existence. It's located in your solar plexus region. It's a chakra of activity – to say the least. It's the source of our power, our inner energy. It's related to our actions, emotional relationships, things we like and dislike. It's a place, where your character is "located" - it's where you want to adjust yourself to the society, achieve goals and dreams, gain power (or at least that manager post).

This chakra is responsible for cleaning the energies of lower chakras – adjust them, and turn them from primeval animal emotions and instincts into creative force, that helps us achieve fulfillment, and achieve happiness – by showing us our true goals and dreams, and not our "animal" needs. Through this chakra, the energies of higher chakras manifest, so we can bring wisdom, love and spirituality to the physical world and our own life.

It's like this chakra translate our basic need of material gain into something more spiritual, so we can (for example) become rich, but at the same time be happy, good towards others, and spiritually developed. Or another example, this chakra change your basic sex instinct into something "more", so your sex is not just physical need, but it is a way of showing love to your partner, and manifesting the power of universal creation forces.

It's also chakra that can help you define others. For example, through this chakra you will sense if another person is positive or negative, as through this chakra, we emit either the light, or the darkness. This light or darkness is our perception of the world, and we can either look on the bright side of life, or the dark side. So others can "sense" you, and you can sense others – if your chakra is open and harmonious, when it will encounter negative energies, it will automatically defend itself by closing, it's a defense mechanism. You will feel scared, threatened. But if you will encounter someone who project light, positive emotions, you will feel warm, pleasant, and safe.

Harmonious Work

When your chakra's work is harmonious, you're at peace, relaxed, and you're harmonized. You're happy because of your life, your job, your family and on, you accept yourself, and you're capable of accepting others as they are. You're kind towards others, and you have strength and energy to achieve your goals and show kindness towards others. You project positive energies, and this protect you against negative vibrations and negative energies.

It's a chakra that can turn law of attraction into a powerful tool – peaceful and happy mind can attract everything it dreams about, period.

Disharmonious Work

You would like to control everything, always have the last word, you would like to gain power, and control people around you. At the same time, you know you're not at peace, and your thoughts and goals are chaotic. You might lack self-confidence;

it's hard for you just to sit down and relax. You might have too many goals, too many dreams, which you're unable to achieve, really, because, instead of searching for peace, you're trying to achieve peace by achieving goals.

But know this – when you will seek peace, the Universe will provide you with answers, and proper goals you're able to achieve.

Blockages

With blockages in the third chakra, you feel sad, depressed, you see only problems and obstacles that make your dreams unachievable. You are closed, and you're hiding your emotions, because you don't want to show them to the world, afraid that people will stop respecting you if you will open yourself. This blocks your energies, and your true power of life.

In result, you might get stomach problems, and you might be afraid of all new problems that might be, you're afraid of new experiences.

NOTE – chakras 1 to 3 are physical chakras – they are related to our physical existence one way or another. 4th chakra is a center for the chakra system, and it's both physical and spiritual. Chakras 5 to 7 are spiritual chakras, related to very abstract things like emotions, or God etc. Therefore, it's hard to describe them with simple words. Sorry about that :).

4th Chakra – Heart - Anahata

Forth chakra is located in your heart. Its standard color is green, and it's a chakra of higher emotions. It is the center of the entire chakra system, a place where 3 lower chakras and 3 higher chakras connect. Sometimes, it's called to be a chakra of physical touch, or movement towards something. It's a chakra of empathy, being able to feel emotions of others, understand others. It's a chakra, through which we admire the beauty of the world, music, art. It's where images, words and sounds are being "translated" into emotions and feelings.

It's the chakra of love – not the physical, but emotional, spiritual love – towards your partner, or entire mankind. It's the place, where pure love exists, love that cannot be destroyed, love that isn't governed by material and physical instincts, but by spiritual forces. Through pure love, we can understand the Source (God), through pure love, we create peace.

It's another chakra, through which we can remove negative blockages, and get rid of negative energies from our life. This chakra teaches you that illnesses and problems can be healed, if you will face your illness and problem with pure love – try this whenever you have a chance. Think about this – you cannot fight the darkness with darkness, you need to light a candle, to fight the darkness of night.

It's important chakra to develop, as it helps us connect with the Source (God), and access our intuitive feelings.

Harmonious Work

Harmonious work of the 4th chakra makes you a channel of positive, pure spiritual energies, love energies. These energies might start changing the world around you, people you're working with, friends, your partner, or family and so on. Your emotions are free of fear and doubt, and you're ready to help people.

You love because you want to love; you give because you wish to give, and you expect nothing in return. And you experience life as purest gift of God – gift of happiness and love.

Disharmonious Work

You expect things in return for your actions, gifts and love. You wish to help people, but you're not using the pure love; instead, you're a victim of your own ego. You're giving and loving because you know you will get something back. You wish people to admire you because you're kind and helpful, but again, it's not a sign of pure love. You might negate your own need for love and higher emotions.

Blockages

You might be dependent on love of others. You might suffer from emotional pain related to love, friendship and relationship. You're sad and depressed. Maybe you wish to give love, but you're afraid that you will be rejected again. Or you might want to give yourself to others because it's what they expect from you, but when someone really needs you, you turn away. You might lack empathy.

5th Chakra – Throat - Vishuddha

This chakra is located in your throat. Its standard color is blue, and it's a chakra of harmony and communication. It's the center of communication, expression of your will and inspiration. Through this chakra, we express ourselves – we express our will, thoughts, point of view, emotions, energies and so on – also, here we express emotions – through laugh, cry, strong words, we speak our minds. We can also express ourselves through books, music, art – these activities are also governed by this chakra. Through this chakra, we show the world what we have inside us – inside all the other chakras.

This chakra gives us the ability of self-reflection, inner sight (not the inner psychic sight, but the ability to analyze our own character). This chakra allows us the ability of objective learning process. Through the development of throat chakra, we learn to separate our thoughts from our emotions and physical feelings, so we can learn the world as it really is. It is another chakra that connects us to the Source, allowing us to tap into our intuition and inspiration.

Harmonious Work

You express your feelings, thoughts and emotions openly. You're not afraid of your weaknesses, and you openly present your strengths. You're capable of expressing yourself, but you can also sit quietly and listen to others. You're not controlled by others, and you're capable of saying "no" if you don't agree with something. You care about your own independence, and you respect the independence of others.

Disharmonious Work

Your actions might be chaotic, disharmonious, and you might behave in a way that is against your inner beliefs. You might be too logical, and too rational, disallowing your emotions and feelings to speak. You're afraid of expressing your true self; you might be afraid of opinion of others. You're hiding your true nature and your weaknesses. You might have a tendency to manipulate others, and your access to subtle planes and information can be blocked. Your spiritual energies might be stuck in your head, so they cannot truly manifest in your life.

Blockages

Once more, you might have problems with expressing yourself. You're either quiet, and you don't talk much, or you talk only about your outer life – your job for, example; you hide your inner emotions and problems. You don't trust people, and you're afraid of their judgment. You do perceive yourself according to their judgment, and you don't trust your own intuition. You might lack self-confidence. You're blind to spiritual powers, and you perceive only the physical world.

6th Chakra – Third Eye - Adjna

The famous third eye is located on your forehead, or as some sources say, between your eyebrows. Its standard color is purple, and it's a chakra of intelligence, mind and psychic powers. It's responsible for conscious learning and understanding the phenomena of existence. Through the Third Eye, we manifest our reality, our thoughts and emotions. Somehow, it's related to the famous law of attraction – every manifestation begins with a thought. But often, our manifestation is a subject to our fears, negative emotions, negative patterns etc, so if you want to attract perfect life, first you need to deal with your blockages. Opening this chakra is important for psychic healing and different forms of psychic readings. It's because, through opened chakra, we can send and receive energies that contain information.

Harmonious Work

Your mind is logical, but capable of intuitive thinking and tapping into intuitive information, as well. You might have good visualization skills. You have good intellectual capabilities. And that's all that I can say, basically. Everything else, that mysterious ability to learn and understand the phenomena of existence, it's hard to describe. I see is in this way – you're awareness expands, you're beginning to see things you haven't seen before – connections between cause and effect, relationship between people and events, ultimate laws of the universe.

Disharmonious Work

You're a person living according to rules of logic and rational thinking, and these are the only rules that you follow; you do not accept your intuition. You have an analytical mind, and you're always looking for rational answer. You fail to accept spiritual knowledge, because you accept only things that can be proved with scientific logical methods.

Blockages

Physical world is the only reality you can accept; your needs are defined by material pursuits and physical needs. Spiritual pursuits bores and troubles you, you reject spiritual knowledge (and you're unable of accepting psychic phenomena as reality). Your thoughts might be dominated by your emotional patterns.

7th Chakra – Crown - Sahasrara

The chakra of spirituality, located on the top of your head (or slightly above your head, according to some sources), its standard color is white, (pearl white), or gold, or bright purple. It's the source of pure, spiritual powers of man. It's where all the energies of lower chakras unite. It's where we are directly connected with the Source (God). It's the chakra of final understanding of life, the universe and everything :). And there's no better way to put it.

Harmonious Work

There are no blockages in the seventh chakra – it can only lack energies. The development of this chakra leads to illumination, (Japanese: Satori), final understanding and new perception of the world around you, as the ultimate creation of God.

Disharmonious Work

If this chakra isn't opened enough, you might see no real purpose of life, and you might be afraid of death, spiritual powers, God. You might become the victim of your own ego.

Chakras Summary

You have learned about the chakras, and now you're ready to move on. For now, this theoretical knowledge will be enough. Later on, I will teach you how to cleanse and open your chakras, so you can develop further. For now, we have other things to discuss.

Energy Channels

Finally, beside energy bodies and chakras, there are energy channels – Meridians. Through these channels, energy flow – it is being delivered to all chakras, and vital organs of your body. If some organs aren't receiving enough energy, this might lead to illnesses. Also, if chakras do not receive enough energies because of the blockages, they won't develop enough, and this will lead to disharmonious work, as described in the chakras section above.

And this completes the second chapter of this book. You've learned about the energy body structure: chakras and energy channels. This knowledge will prove to be useful in the future, especially in case of emotional healing.

The Mind Work

"To the mind that is still, the whole universe surrenders."

Meditation

I'm sure you're already tired with the theory. But we're not done yet. Still, it is time to learn some practical skill, at least. Meditation, as this is the skill which I'm talking about, is important in any psychic or spiritual practice. Your mind is your primary tool in psychic awakening. It must be calm and focused. Meditation gives many benefits, and calm mind is just a minor thing. But let's discuss subconscious blockages, first. At least one more time.

The Nature Of Blockages

So what are these energy blockages, again? Blockages are energies stuck in energy channels (Meridians). Think of it like of plugged water pipes – water cannot flow freely through the pipe, so it can't reach your home – and you suffer because you have no access to water. The same thing happens in case of psychic energies. Energies that are blocking energy channels block the free flow of life energies; thus, they cannot reach vital body cells, nor they can reach your chakras. As you know from the previous lesson, this can result in both physical and emotional problems. Let's throw a simple example. Blockage on a meridian leading to your sacral chakra can result in problems with sex. Simple.

How are such blockages created? They are created when you're subject to low-vibration energies. By low-vibration energies, I mean negative emotions – fear, hate, anger, sadness, enviousness, stress and so on. These emotions are parts of negative patterns, like:

- **Stereotypes** – take racism, for example, when you consider someone a thug because of the color of his skin, then it's negative pattern, you're intolerant towards this person. Intolerance is low vibration energy, negative emotion.
- **Negative knowledge** – when parents or teachers teach you that life is difficult, or people are not to be trusted, or that you should shut up, and dump your creativity, this creates negative pattern, as you are being taught that the world is awful – this leads to negative emotions, and of course, blockages.
- **Life trauma** – if your heart have been broken, if you have lost a family member, if you have being raped, or bitten, then you suffer from serious negative emotions.

- **Hate** – hate is a result of life trauma of some sort, but by projecting hate, by hating someone, you create additional blockages.

Anything that is somehow connected to negative emotions, can create negative pattern, thus energy blockage. But also positive emotions can create patterns – in this case, when you're happy to allow someone to control your life, you create a pattern, through which you allow someone to drain your energies, or to fill you with negative energies. Happiness and acceptance towards crimes opens the door towards negative energies. Openness towards psychic vampires opens them the door to suck you out. And so on – so as you can see, not only negative emotions can be dangerous, but also positive emotions. Still – blockages are created only by negative emotions (you will learn how to close yourself to the influence of others soon, don't worry).

Low vibration energies, caused by negative emotions, have a tendency to be stuck – only positive, spiritual energy flows freely through your energy system, or through the environment. Negative energies stuck – they create places of negativity (such as haunted homes, that aren't really haunted), and they stuck within your energy channels. These low-vibration energies are like bad cholesterol that leads to heart attack. They block vital energies – your Chi. And without Chi, your chakras can't develop enough, and their work is disharmonious. The only real way to allow more energies to flow into the chakras, and develop them – thus pushing your psychic and spiritual development further – is to clear the blockages.

This can be done through either energy work, or mind work. Energy work is pure energy manipulation. You use your will to direct psychic energies through energy channels into the chakras, to destroy the blockages. But this can be dangerous at first, as it's not a gentle method – it's much safer to use energy manipulation to deal with your blockages after you have learned how to use your mind programming abilities to work gently with your blockages, than it is to practice energy work without this knowledge. These gentle methods are affirmations and emotional healing. They can be used to deal with the blockages that you are aware of.

But some blockages are hidden – you don't remember all your traumatic experiences, or negative emotions, bad episodes of your life, right? That's why there are also additional methods to help negative patterns and blockages to re-emerge. These methods are energy work, and breathing techniques that are directly related to the energy flow. You will learn about breathe techniques later. For now, know this – before you start re-emerging your blockages and patterns, you need to know how to deal with them first. That's why now you're going to learn about meditation, prayer, affirmations and emotional healing. By learning these methods, you will be prepared to deal with all the problems that might re-emerge later, during your psychic awakening.

What Are The Effects Of Removing Blockages?

By removing blockages, even within few weeks after you start your practice, you might start to experience your intuition kicking in, your psychic sensitivity increasing, and after a month or two, your third eye might be opened enough, to allow you to start performing basic psychic readings. But again – do not expect anything to happen – you will learn about all these fancy psychic abilities in another lesson, in the second half of this Psychic Awakening Course. I'm mentioning this, because I want you to know the fact – don't be surprised if you will start to know things before they happen, or sense emotions of people, or sense if something is filled with positive or negative energies. Don't be surprised, but at the same time, do not expect it to happen. Expectations can create additional energy blockages, so be at peace – relax, expect nothing, and observe.

So psychic abilities kicking in is just the first thing that you might experience after working with your negative patterns. Another thing is more "earthly" - you might feel more at peace, you might be more relaxed, you might feel happy, just like that. You might be calmer, and in intense situations, you might react with peace, not aggression. You might stop worrying about simple problems. You might – I'm using this world, because it's hard to say when you will experience these things – at some point, you will, but some people will experience peace after a month of practice, some people will experience peace after years of practice. Again – expect nothing, and keep practicing.

Why Do Mind Techniques Work?

Why do affirmations, meditation and emotional healing methods works in case of energy blockages? You have learned earlier, that your etheric body is connected to the astral body, and astral body is directly connected to your subconscious – subconscious is the place, where your negative patterns are stored. By using your conscious mind to delete patterns from subconscious, you delete patterns from the astral body, and thus, you allow the etheric energy blockages to be removed, as well. Et voila – it's that simple. Now when you understand what energy blockages are, you will start to learn how to deal with them, so they won't block your own development. You will start by learning meditation.

Meditation – Zazen practice

First step towards dealing with energy blockages is learning how to meditate. Often, many courses, books and many workshops present meditation as a method of putting your mind at peace, releasing stress and developing psychic abilities. Indeed, it's true. Meditation serves multiple purposes:

- First of all, through meditation you learn how to observe consciously your thoughts – and among these thoughts, there are also fears, expectations and negative patterns. By peaceful observation, you relax the tensions that accompany these patterns, and it's a step to healing the emotions, thus releasing the blockages. As you will learn later, it's a method similar to healing your emotions. Therefore, it's the reason why meditation is the first step towards dealing with your blockages.
- You also expand your awareness – you learn how to be aware of your thoughts, your physical sensations, and your environment. This leads to the ability of being aware of intuitive thoughts, and energies around you.

Finally, you learn how to observe everything around you with peaceful and calm emotions. Thus, meditation turns to be the basic and most important ability which you can use for your psychic awakening.

In this book, I will teach you the way of Zazen and few other, simpler techniques, as well. Let's start with Zazen. It's a meditation school that originates from Zen Buddhism. It's not religious practice, but mind practice that doesn't require any prayers to any entity. All you need is 25 minutes of peace each day. First, I will describe the Zazen practice with words, and then you can watch the instructional video for this lesson.

NOTE: If you have the opportunity to learn Zazen in a temple, or on Zen workshops, do so. In many countries, and many cities, Zen practice is available to everyone who is willing to learn. Different books and different teachers will teach you slightly different methods of Zazen – but the principle is the same – sit down, relax, clear your mind and just sit still and observe.

Zazen How-To

First, you need to prepare the room for meditation. Make sure no one will disturb you for the next half an hour. Don't worry about any candles, incenses or special tools – none of this is required in Zazen. Zazen is a practice that works with your mind, and not any tools like magick candles and such. Because you're not going to practice during a workshop or in a temple, or room prepared specially for Zazen practice, you might need to improvise.

Zazen is "sitting", so you need something to sit on. You need a large pillow which you're going to flex in such way, that when you sit on it, your buttocks are placed about 10 up to 20 centimeters above the ground. Or you can use a blanket, flex it the same way. The point is that your buttocks should be higher than your knees, because when you're going to sit in Lotus position, it will make your sitting easier. You can find online stores, where you can purchase special pillows for meditation – I believe they are called "Zafu". If you like, you can purchase such pillow, as it should make your sitting even easier. But as I said, if you don't have access to such store, or you're out of money currently, then improvise. It's what I do constantly :).

You also need a blank wall to face. By blank, I mean that it should have no pictures hanging, no paintings, no furniture near and so on. If you can't find such wall, then choose the "blankest" part of your room, where there will be little distractions for your conscious mind. This is meant to lower the possibility of distractions. Of course, you are not obligated to practice in a closed room, you can choose your garden, park, ocean shore, forest or anything like this. The choice is yours, but at first, start your practice at home, to learn the basics of Zazen.

Sitting Practice

Prepare your "pillow", and sit on it with your legs crossed in Lotus position. It doesn't really matter which leg will be on top, what really matters is that left foot should be on your right thigh, and right foot on your left thigh. Make sure your spine is straight, and put your hands together into the mudra, like on the image below. Fingers of the right palm lies on the fingers of the left palm, and your thumbs touch together above. Place your hands near your Tan Tien, it's where your second chakra is located, few centimeters below your navel. This area is called "Hara". We're mixing terms here a little, as Hara is not the same thing as chakra. Chakras are terms that originate in Hindu system, while Hara is a Japanese term, that is a result of mixture of Buddhism and Taoism. But don't worry about this, just keep reading and learning.

Illustration 2: Touch Your Hands Like This

Illustration 3: Zazen Sitting Meditation

Use the images below for additional reference regarding sitting. When your hands touch each other, when you sit in Lotus position, and your spine is strength, you can learn how to breathe.

NOTE: The matter of straight spine is important, but I understand that a lot of people who live in mode world might have troubles sitting with straight spine. Personally, I have spinal defect that makes sitting for more than 2 minutes with straight spine very hard. But do your best!

Yet, do not worry if you will bend your spine a little – the real point behind sitting is mind work, not the perfect pose. I remember learning meditation myself. I couldn't understand how can people sit still for an hour and more, until I understood that most modern guides for Western people were written by "copy/paste" method, and the authors didn't know that it's impossible to sit still for 5 minutes and more in proper meditation pose with spine defect.

So, when you're having problems with your spine, don't worry about perfect pose. Consult your doctor and consult they way you can sit, then improvise.

Sitting still, you can now begin your practice. But first, take a look down – I mean, with your head straight, pull your chin back, and lower your sight, look at the floor or wall that is about one meter in front of you. Do not bend your hand to look down, just use your eyes. And here's an important thing – do not close your eyes. Zazen is an art of meditation with eyes open. Keep that in mind. But of course, you can blink. When you will be starring down, after few minutes your vision might begin to blur – this is bad. I mean, it's very normal, but the point is to focus and discipline yourself. When your vision begins to change, discipline your sense, consciously focus to see clearly again.

Next step is your breath. When you sit, take a breath in, and push your diaphragm outwards. When you breath out, pull your diaphragm inwards. This is diaphragm breathing, and for most people, it will be difficult at first, but keep practicing, as you need to learn proper breath method. Without it, your meditation will be incomplete. Breath it, and breath out, slowly and gently.

Your breath is the tool to keep focused. When you breath it, start counting – say in your mind "first", in to parts. When your breath in, say "fir", and when you breath out, say "st" - expand each number for the entire breath-in-breath-out process, so you will sense the continuity of your count. Count from 1 to 10, like this "first, second, third, fourth" and so on. And when you will reach 10, start all over from "first". And continue to breath and count.

And that's basically it – you have learned how to practice Zazen. Continue your meditation up to 25 minutes per day, it will be enough. Of course if you want, you can practice longer, it's your choice. But 25 minutes are a minimum. Now, that you know how to "sit", you can learn how to use Zazen to clear your mind.

Observation Of Thoughts

When you sit there for 25 minutes or longer, breathing and starring on the wall, or floor, many thoughts will "pop up" out of nowhere. That "nowhere" is your subconscious, and these thoughts are the thoughts that are currently shaping your life. You can notice thoughts about the even last night, the email you had received an hour ago, or an event that shaped your life 20 years ago and so on. All you have to do is to observe these thoughts.

Many meditation techniques suggest that, but rarely anyone explains what that observation really do. It's all about healing your emotions. Getting rid of negative patterns and memories, emotions and blockages is simple – you need to start perceiving all the negativity of the specific event as a neutral observer. Only then, the blockage will be removed, and the emotions of the specific event in question won't govern your life. And they can govern – if you have been told that money are hard to get, for many years you might suffer from financial problems. By removing the blockage, and healing the emotions of the event (for example, the day your dad screamed at you, telling you that it's hard to earn money), within weeks you might notice that your financial situation is getting better.

Zazen can heal emotions – by switching your emotional state from aggressive or sad, into neutral. That's why you need to observe your thoughts with peace, with a calm mind, observe them like neutral observer. Don't force them to go away, don't try to hide them, do not try to silence your emotions. Just remain calm and observe. That's all. Counting and breathing is a way to keep your mind focused, and calm, so you can observe things peacefully, with no emotions.

Gentle observation will cause memories to go away gently. These thoughts will be replaced with new thoughts, then new thoughts will go away and so on. At some point – after weeks or months, you will notice that your mind is calmer and that thoughts do not pop up any more, or that they are very rare. And that will benefit in your daily life – with your relationship, job, friendship, family life and of course, with your psychic development, as well.

So sit still, breathe, count and observe your thoughts and emotions.

Additional Tips For Meditation

Zazen is simple after few days of practice behind you. I have few more tips for you. First, meditation is a great way to charge your crystals with positive, spiritual energies. You're going to use quartz crystals in this psychic awakening course, so now learn your first method of charging them. Meditation attracts positive, spiritual energies, and quartz crystals have a tendency to collect psychic energies. Put them around you during your Zazen, and they will be charged to some point with positive energies. You should try this method after a month or two months of meditation, because at first, you might project negative energies, that will be leaving your etheric body. You don't want crystals charged with negativity :).

At first, I said that you need 30 minutes of peace – 5 minutes to prepare yourself, 25 minutes for meditation. But don't worry, if there will be loud music playing in your neighbors flat. Or that your siblings will make noise. Or that your partner will cook dinner and so on. Actually, such distractions are helpful, as thanks to them, you learn how to focus more, and you improve your concentration. This is a great way to learn additional control over your mind and emotions. Zazen is a great way to improve your focus abilities, and focus is important in many psychic practices.

You have learned how to practice Zazen. From now on, spend at least 3 days each week meditating for 25 minutes. Personally, I meditate on 2 pm, between work time and development time, but you can choose any time of the day. Many teachers suggest meditating in the early morning, or late evening just before sunset – indeed, during these times of the day, energies are very strong. But if you don't have time in the morning or in the evening, then any free 25 minutes will do the job.

Practice meditation from now on. With time, it will become your daily habit, and you won't be able to live without it. Learning meditation is an important step in your psychic awakening. Once again, do not expect any results, just focus on practicing. After few weeks, and surely after few months, you will notice a difference in your life. How big it will be, it depends on the time you spent practicing, and your other practices like affirmations, or emotional healing.

Spend at least one more week changing your diet habits, and taking short or long walks, this time add meditation practice. Make sure you breath and count correctly, and you calmly observe your thoughts.

Other Methods Of Meditation

If you followed carefully words in the previous paragraph, you already know what meditation is really about - it's all about focus. And even if I recommend Zazen as your primary meditation practice, some people might prefer simpler methods for a good start. So, below you will find simpler meditation techniques.

Sit down in armchair, lie on your bed or on the floor. Make sure you're comfortable, really make sure of this, because you're going to spend few minutes in this position. Now close your eyes and do not move. Count down from 40 to 0 quietly in your mind, breathe deeply and slowly, do not think about anything, but when pictures do appear in front of your eyes, just acknowledge them and ignore, moving forward. When you reach 0, it's time to get to work. Think of an orange - of it's color, smell, taste, texture. Try to "feel" it with your fingers, "smell" it and "taste" it - if you have ever eaten an orange, you do remember the smell and taste, try to imagine these now. And when you're done, keep focused on these elements for few minutes - the longer the better. When you're done, open your eyes. When you will open them, you will already be a beginner psychic, because you will already know meditation. See? It's that simple!

You can meditate on different things - your current day, your friend, the dinner, or you can just enjoy the feelings reaching you in this meditation state; or you can observe the pictures coming to your mind, maybe there's a message out there for you? Imagine a Zen monk, or master Yoda from Star Wars sitting and not moving for few hours, meditating - isn't this cool?

Zazen teaches you how to clear your mind. Clearing your mind allows you to pick up only those information you need - in this case, psychic data. Below are additional techniques of meditation – they will teach you how to clear your mind, and how to focus on nothingness.

Meditation Technique #1

In order to focus on nothingness, begin the above meditation exercise. Count down from 40 0, but this time, do not think of an orange. Actually, do not think about anything in particular, instead focus on a small point in the very center of your head, somewhere deep in your brain. Literally feel this small dot inside and keep focused on it at all time. Do this for at least 15 minutes per each meditation session. If you will get distract or you will catch yourself thinking of something, just acknowledge it, and focus on again. With time, you will be able to focus more intensively and for longer. And you will find out you can focus on that point any time you want. This is an important skill which is called "centering" and it will be discussed later when we finally get to the part talking about energy body.

This meditation, this talent will help you focus not just for psychic work, but also for any other task during your day - learning, working, even cooking or reading a book for pleasure. It's a great example that psychic development is useful not only for psychic readings for your neighbors and friends.

Meditation Technique #2

For some people, the first technique of meditation might not work. I recognize the problems. That's why here's another technique you can try if the first one didn't feel "good" enough. Nearly everything is the same beside the very beginning.

Sit down comfortable and close your eyes. Start counting from 1 to 30 (so as you can see, it's a little different technique than previous one). Breath deeply, and when you reach 5, focus on the sound of your breath. On 10, focus on your heart bit – either the sound, of pulsing sensation within your body. On 15 relax completely, let go all tensions. On 20, clear your mind of all thoughts. At 25 focus on the darkness in front of your eyes. When you reach 30, simple meditate – focus on emptiness, or specific task.

Yep, the focus is not just about emptiness, if you want you can focus on other things, as well. For example, I like to use meditation in order to "program" some behavior in my mind, such as anger control. Or you can meditate on the problem, or person you have met etc.

Now, when you already know how to meditate, we can move forward. Do you want to learn more about meditation? Search for books on meditation system, like Taoist meditation or Hindu Vipassana system. Taoist meditation focus more on energy work and manipulating psionic energies through primary energy channel, while Vipassana focus on "thinking of nothing" - and those are only two general techniques of meditation, with enough exploration you will learn about many other, very different from each other, meditation systems.

A Matter Of Trance

I have to mention something that many psychic teachers or books advice – a trance. Trance is an altered state of mind, in which you shut down nearly all of your physical senses in order to focus on one thing. And one thing only. In many systems and practices, it's a way of contacting the spirit word.

Trance is such a popular psychic technique. Books and teachers tell you that you need to enter a trance state in order to acquire psychic information. Sufficient to say, this is a misleading opinion. I can perform chakra reading while jogging - I just need clear mind, not any form of trance. To be honest, you must know that trance only limits your perception, making you blind to many psychic impressions and intuitive thoughts. Clearing your mind is your goal, and this can be accomplished through meditation techniques explained above. No trance is needed if you want to become psychic.

It is my believe that you should not practice trance states. I was experimenting with them, but I have to admit, that my psychic development speed increased when I finally gave up my trance practices. Trance is useless, to say the least. And it's not a real psychic path. Awareness is. So, please, don't play with trance, because it leads nowhere.

Meditation is never about shutting all your senses, and blocking your contact with the physical reality. Meditation is about awareness, and psychic potential is about awareness. Begin aware of information, energies, impressions, intuitive thoughts etc, is what makes you psychic. Shutting down your senses during trance is not. An argument, commonly posted by 'trance maniacs' is that trance state allows people to manifest their dreams, or tap into messages from astral planes. Well, peaceful and disciplined mind can achieve the same thing, and you don't have to enter any trance states.

There's no point of wasting your time on learning trance. Just focus on classic meditation.

Other Ways Of Dealing With Blockages

Meditation is just one of many ways to work out your blockages. You're going to learn more about dealing with blockages now, and in addition, you will learn a bit about prayers and forgiveness. These are powerful tools in the hands of a psychic, and they will serve your psychic awakening well.

Prayer

Prayer is something that is present in almost every single religion and/or culture. It is a conversation with God, and I strongly emphasize the word "conversation" - you speak, then you listen and God speak. There is a saying that when you speak with God, you're religious, and when God speak to you, you're mentally ill – this is (mostly) true, but the fact is – your intuition, your higher psychic self, this is your connection to the Source. Through your intuition, and your inner psychic self, God, or The Source, speaks to you, sending your thoughts, inspirations, information and advices.

Prayer is very important and useful tool of a psychic. First, thanks to prayer you can ask the Source for things. And through prayer, you can receive answers, simple. What kind of things can you ask? Well – what do you want to ask for? Protection? Advices? Ideas? It will be simpler if I will give you examples from my own practice.

> *I often ask for protection when I do psychic readings, or I ask for cleansing when I feel I'm surrounded by negative energies. I ask for permission if I'm going to do psychic reading, and I ask if I can perform the reading at all (sometimes I'm not allowed to).*
> *I ask for inspirations regarding my business – I ask for help regarding promotion of my websites and services. I ask for strength, so I can pass over difficult financial time. I ask for advices regarding my goals.*
> *I ask if I should visit "that" specific haunted place (it's my hobby).*
> *During Reiki practice, I ask where should I apply energy, and how to deal with health problems, or how to relieve pain.*
> *And of course, during psychic readings, I ask for information which I'm supposed to pass to the person I read.*

As you can see, during prayer you can ask for many things – not necessary spiritual, but very earthly as well – such as financial issues, or inspirations etc.

How To Pray

How to pray, actually? First of all, you're not praying towards any person – you don't pray to any saint, or spirit, or ghost, or angel, or a guru or anyone like this – you pray to God, to the Source, to the Absolute. But you don't really need to believe in God – think about it like about the law of attraction – you ask the Universe for something, and it replies, one way or another. Don't consider your prayer as religious practice but as spiritual practice.

You don't pray with written prayer like Lord's Prayer, or anything like this. You pray with your own words – and using your heart, not your brain. You need to feel the words you're pronouncing; you need to feel the emotions. Otherwise, the prayer is useless, or at least, it has a lesser impact. Don't think you need to use correct or appropriate words, speak your mind and relax – don't be worried, the Boss above doesn't care about the words you're using, the Boss cares about your intention and your positive emotions.

Feel positive emotions, and recognize that prayer is a spiritual practice. But at the same time, relax – don't think that you're doing something wrong, or that the time is wrong, or the place is wrong. If you want, you can pray during rush hour sitting in a bus, stuck in a traffic jam. Prayer is our natural activity, and we should consider it spiritual practice, but we shouldn't consider it so sacred that it should be performed only in a sacred place during sacred ritual.

Below, you can see few examples of my prayers:

Boss, am I allowed to scan this person's chakras?

Boss, please send me inspirations regarding new useful article for A State of Mind.

Boss, help me cleanse these negative energies that surround my aura.

As you can see, these are simple prayers, using simple words. Nothing too fancy. One more thing – at the end of each prayer, say "thank you" - or at least "thanks" - and really be thankful. After all, you're asking for something – it's nice to say thanks :).

How To Listen?

Praying is one thing – listening is another. After asking the question, whether you seek advices, inspirations, or help, you need to listen. The answer might come in different ways. Sometimes, it can arrive through intuition directly – you just know the answer. Sometimes, it can arrive in a dream. Or as cool tune in the radio. Or someone you will be talking with, might say something that will prove to be the answer to your question. Or maybe you will sense physical effects of energy cleansing you.

The answer doesn't have to come instantly – it might arrive within seconds, or within weeks, or even months. Know this – The Source always replies, but some people just can't listen. So observe all coincidences that will happen to you, and all your thoughts, actions, conversations and experiences – somewhere there is the answer you seek.

Pray often – it's your privilege, your way of communicating with the Source.

The Source And Protection

This is what I mentioned when I discussed working with ghosts and spirits in the previous chapter. You can use a prayer for very serious thing – prayer of protection. It's quite simple – before you enter a haunted place; or head for paranormal investigation; or read any spiritual book; or seek new teacher, ask the Source if you should really do this, for example: Boss, I'm going to ask this man to teach me about psychic abilities. Should I do this? Will be I safe?

And then, just ask for an answer. And if the Boss says that you shouldn't do something, listen to your intuition. You will be much safer this way. You can use this simple prayer of protection before paranormal investigations, teacher meeting, new development workshop, giving psychic reading or psychic healing. You will save yourself a lot of troubles just by asking this simple question: "is it OK for me to do this?"

Forgiveness

Forgiveness is another great tool in hands of psychic. This tool can be used for additional mind work, to deal with blockages and negative patterns in your subconscious. Many traumas and emotional problems are caused by negative events, and we often associate negative events or teachings with people. Almost automatically, we're starting to hate or at least dislike people we perceive as reasons of all our problems. And this creates problems.

Forgiveness is useful because once we forgive the person, the negative pattern related to that person cannot exist anymore. And although problems related to the person might still exist, they are much easier to get rid of, once the negative emotions towards the person has been dealt with. So forgive people you think are the source of your problems. Just like that – say in your mind that you "forgive John for bitting me in High School" - or something like that :). It's so simple!

Forgive people who caused you pain, people who taught you negative patterns and so on. You will feel much lighter.

Also, forgive yourself. You might have made many mistakes in your life – you might have lied, steal, hurt people, feel shame or stupid. It's time to let it go. Forgive yourself that you hurt someone, forgive that you have stolen the book from the local library, forgive yourself that you acted stupid while that girl looked at you, forgive that you were lazy and so on.

Forgiving yourself won't change the past – but at least will change your habits and your subconscious patterns. Pain of the past shapes your future, and it controls it. If you wish to gain control over your life, then you need to understand that the past is something you leave behind. It happened, get over it and move on! You will feel much better if the pain of the past won't control you anymore. And forgiving yourself is the first step in relieving this pain.

The more you forgive – either others or yourself – the more blockages will be removed, the easier the energy will flow. I don't need to remind that it is causing your psychic awakening, right?

Exercise - Improving Your Focus & Patience

In the meantime, I want to get back to the subject of patience and focus. You're already improving your focus and patience through Zazen meditation (you are meditating, aren't you?), but if you want, you can use additional exercise to do so – it's candle staring. You need to place a candle in a dark room, and light it. Then sit down within two meters from the candle, relax and start staring at the candle flame. Continue staring for next 5, 10, 15 minutes and practice the exercise until you will be able to stare at the flame for at least 30 minutes. When you're able to stare at the flame for 30 minutes few days in a row, you can stop practicing this exercise. As I said, it's an additional exercise, and Zazen meditation will be enough, but if you want more, you can try this exercise, as well.

Anyway, now I have homework for you, again. From now on, start praying. Pray for:

1. **Inspirations** – regarding your life, future, work, hobby, relationship.
2. **Growth** – psychical, spiritual, intellectual.

3. **Protection** – during psychic practice, or on a daily basis.

Or for anything else you wish. You don't have to pray daily – but if you're in need, don't be afraid to ask the Source for help. And remember that it doesn't matter what your religion is – just start praying to your spiritual master – God, deity etc. with your heart, not your brain.

Next, make a list of people who hurt or influenced you somehow in the past, and forgive them – one person at the time. Truly forgive the person, feel the relief, relax and be at peace. Then move to another person. You don't need to forgive everyone at once. You can follow the list for next few weeks or even months if you prefer. Take your time, and forgive the person when you're ready.

Finally, make a list of reasons to forgive yourself for – any problems you caused, people you hurt, things you did or felt etc. And again, start forgiving yourself, one thing at the time. Take your time, psychic development is not a race, it's gentle growth. Spend at least one week forgiving people and yourself.

Intuition

At some point of your development, as I already mentioned earlier, you will awake your intuition. Or should I say, you will awake your ability to contact the Source through intuition. It will happen sooner or later. By "The Source", you can understand many things, as I already mentioned. Personally, I understand God, an Absolute, the Universe, the universal power of creation. But if you prefer, you can consider the Source to be some higher power, spiritual force, or your higher psychic self. In any case, your intuition allows you to be psychic - because being psychic, at least on the level of Extra Sensory Perception, is all about receiving and channeling information from the Source - whatever it is.

Your psychic intuition is in reality an ability to know things - to receive information through various means, for example, as images, sounds, or just by knowing the information as instant thought. To better understand intuition, I will post an example from my own psychic practice.

I use to ask the Source if I'm allowed to perform psychic reading for a specific person. And I receive an answer through my intuition. In most cases, it's just an instant thought that I "know" - yes or no.

And that's it - this is your intuition. Intuition is an ability to acquire information through psychic means. In most cases, you know the answer as thought. Sometimes, you can receive audio information. Sometimes, visual information as images, pictures, scenes or symbols, this is clairvoyance. And sometimes you can sense things with your physical body as touch, warm, cold, or tension. Intuition is your inner voice that guides you. It doesn't tell you what to do, but it only provides you with tips, guidelines and information that might be useful at the time.

How To Use Your Intuition

Your intuition can be used in a variety of ways. Mainly, you will use it for different forms of psychic abilities, like psychometry or psychic readings, in order to get answers to your "control questions", and receive information about objects and people. Basically, you need to ask for information, and you need to listen to information.

And you ask for information by asking for it with your thoughts, simple with your. Intend - think what do you want to know right now... And then listen to the answer. Answers come in a variety of ways, as I already have said. And basically, this is it, there's no fancy guide to listening to your intuition, but one word - practice. At first you might not be able to use your intuition correctly, but with time and practice, you will develop your ability to listen to that inner voice.

You might ask "how do I know that the answer I have received comes from the Source, and not from me?" - well, you don't. First of all, it's hard to tell if we're contacting the Source, or if psychic powers originate from our higher mind only. Second of all, you're never sure until you get confirmations from other people, and from events and experiences. And at some point, you will just learn to different both types of information - it will be a gentle difference, that cannot be described with words - you must feel it. But with time, and more proofs that your intuition is correct, you will learn.

Just start using your gut feelings – it's your intuition, your primary psychic ability. When you will learn how to listen to it, every single psychic ability like psychic reading, psychometry, remote viewing etc. will be just a matter of understanding how can you apply your intuition in your daily life. And when you will awake your intuition, then you will be able to say - "I'm psychic now".

Make a note in your journal

From now on, write down all your predictions, thoughts, hunches and events when you just "know things" before they happen. If your feelings confirm, mark it, but when you're wrong, also mark it. This way you will have additional way of learning which predictions come true, and which doesn't, and how does real intuitive thought "feels" like.

Also, writing down your psychic experiences teaches your subconscious that this is what you want, and you want to experience more of these psychic events.

Awakening your intuition is a huge step forward in your psychic development, even if your ability to listen is just beginning to emerge. Why is it so? Because you can use your intuition in so many ways - you can use it for psychic readings, and psychometry, but also for receiving guidance regarding your business, financial issues, relationship, family life, friends, job, traffic jam. Do not think that it is inappropriate to use intuition and psychic abilities in business. First of all, life on planet Earth have a lot in common with money, and second of all, if your intentions are pure and positive, the Source will have no objections and it will help you.

Personally, I do listen to my intuition regarding business issues, and so far, the Source has never let me down. You can do it, as well.

Intuitive Progress

When your intuition will kick in, you might start to notice that you're having problems with some exercises and paths of your development. For example, you might be worry that what you're practicing is wrong and that you should do something else. Or you might feel that you need to change your diet. Or you might even feel that this book is no longer meant for you. As much as I would like you to finish it, and recommend it to your friends, I have to tell this - if your intuition tells you to do something, do it! If it tells you to stop reading, then stop reading!

Maybe you're not ready for some of the exercises I have published. Maybe you're not ready for this knowledge at all, and your intuition wants you to work out some negative thought patterns first, so you can return to this book later. No matter what, listen to your intuition - it's channeling guidance from the Source, and the Source wants all the best for you.

Intuitive Exercises

Beside using your intuition in deciding what is good, and what isn't good for you, I have another idea which you may use in your psychic development. Your psychic intuition can help you in designing your psychic exercises, as well. Because all the answers you seek, lies within, only you know what is best for your own growth. Although there are many exercises to follow and to perform in this book, sometimes you might feel that you should practice something else. Your psychic intuition is a powerful tool to do so.

When I was beginning my pendulum practice, I was following guidelines from books regarding the way the pendulum should be hold. Years later, when I moved into more occult studies than simple psychic development, I have find out that my pendulum doesn't work again. Recently, I managed to regain this ability once more, simple by following my intuition. It told me how to hold the pendulum, how to ask questions, what does the swings means etc. I was no longer using books to gain this knowledge, as the written knowledge was... "forbidden" in my case, and it was no longer working. But my intuitive knowledge helped me in my pendulum practice more than any book.

Another time, I was trying to design an exercise to energize my chakras. So I sat down, and I visualized myself as I performed the exercise. And I let go my imagination. I let my intuition guide me in my visualization process. First I saw a background, full of trees, green grass. I quickly identified it as a city park. Then I saw myself as I inhale, and, at the same time, draw the energy through my first chakra. Then I saw myself exhaling and releasing negative energies along with my breath. Then I saw myself as I repeat the process few more times, one breath per each chakra. My intuition guided me to design an exercise for my own psychic development, an exercise that was quite useful for me at the time.

You can do the same, just by closing your eyes, and letting your imagination be guided by your psychic intuition. Just by observing things that come to your mind, it is enough to find out new ways of development. Ways that can be completely different from the techniques from this book. For some readers, awaken intuition might suggest you to switch to your own exercises before you will even get to New Energy Ways chapter. Thus, this book will become just a reference for further studies and inspirations. Other readers might have to read the entire book, and their intuition will kick in later. As I have already mentioned, there are no guidelines, and you should expect nothing.

You will know when it's time for change – just like that.

Now when you have learned a bit more about your intuition, you can start a real fight against negative thought patterns. "You must unlearn what you have learned" - this statement applies like no other to this process of reprogramming your mind, habits, behavior and thought patterns. The chapters that follow, regarding affirmations and emotional healing has been originally published on my website, A State Of Mind, and for this day, they are free to read on-line. I've decided to publish them for free because they're useful, they present powerful tools that can help people in both psychic and spiritual growth. They've been included here because you don't want to jump from a book to a website, right?

Affirmations

Do you know what affirmations are? Basically, an affirmation is a phrase which we can repeat constantly, and this repetition process is meant to reprogram our mind, for example, we can use affirmations to change our negative habit into positive habit. But affirmations are more than this – they're powerful manifestation tools, especially in the hands of skillful psychic.

Still, a lot of people think that it's sufficient just to repeat an affirmation in your mind in order to get it to work. This isn't entirely true. Yes - repeating affirmation in your mind will work, but only if you will repeat it for few months or even years. A good affirmation should be written down, and it should be written down correctly. What does it mean? Look at the example below, please:

I don't have a headache.

If you will repeat this in your mind, then it's affirmation, but it's negative affirmation. Why? Because your subconscious mind, upon which we're trying to operate through this technique, doesn't recognize negation. It doesn't understand the word "not" or "no". To your subconscious, the affirmation above looks like this:

I have a headache.

Simple as that, your subconscious doesn't care if you want or do not want, if you have or do not have. So when you want to start working with affirmations, you need to pay attention now, as there are few things you need to learn first.

How To Create Good Affirmations

First of all, good affirmation must keep thinking in a positive way. It cannot include any negative words or phrases. Below are few examples of bad affirmations:

I don't have a headache.
I'm not worried.

Instead, you should create affirmations that say "my head feels good and OK", "I'm calm and secured". An affirmation must be always positive, in order to replace any negative pattern you might have stored in your subconscious mind. Below are more examples of good affirmations:

I, Nathan, am happy.
I, Nathan, am innocent – if someone is accusing you.
I, Nathan, work efficiently and I like my job – if you have problems in workplace.
I, Nathan, experience pleasure each and every day.

I, Nathan, have the right to feel safe in my home – if you feel threaten.

Quite simple, isn't it? Generally, as I've stated earlier, we create negative patterns throughout our entire life. Emotional traumas, scary events, bad experiences, they all creates our behavior habits, and some of the habits we just can't stand. Affirmations are one of the methods to reprogram our mind, and change negative habits and negative thoughts, into positive habits and positive thoughts.

Notice there's always "*I, NAME, something*" – it's an affirmation for you, so it should include your name – remember, it's a tool to work with your subconscious, and your subconscious need a name for identification. Just stick to this rule.

Let's say you're always tired at work – but you do like your work, you do what you love, yet you don't experience that energy burst some people have. You might figure our it's because few years earlier, you were working in a place you didn't like, and you lost your interest in any kind of work. This is a negative habit I'm talking about. You can now use affirmation to reprogram your mind. Simple by focusing on "I'm always full of energy during work time" you can become a walking power cell one more.

Interesting fact is that affirmations are tools to work with your subconscious, and your subconscious is a nasty pet. For example, if you will change that affirmation a little into "I'm always full of energy in my workplace", then it will work, as well. But notice the keyword workplace – now what might happen if your boss will send you for a delegation? You're no longer in your workplace, and your energy might decide to take a break . Another reason to pay close attention to your keywords.

As I said, affirmations are tools to work with your subconscious. If you focus on each affirmation, and you focus on it with your heart and brain, after few days, perhaps few weeks or months, it starts to overwrite your previous subconscious pattern. It's like a mechanical way to deal with these subconscious problems. Personally, I use affirmations to deal with problems I cannot identify as core images, so I can't work with them with my standard practice.

The best way to explain how affirmations really work will be to give you simple example from my own practice. I had problems with money. I wanted to make more money from my own businesses, but I was just unable to. Some inner growth practices have pointed me to the source of the problem. I had that negative pattern in my mind that was constantly telling me two things:

- First, something that others have taught me in the past – that it's hard to earn money.
- Second, something I had taught myself – that those who are rich, are dishonest assholes.

So I had to deal with these negative patterns. First one was telling me that I can't really make money easy and with pleasure. Second one was even more problematic – how can I become rich if I consider everyone who is rich as asshole? Well, I've created two affirmations: "I, Nathan, make money easy and with pleasure" and "I, Nathan, have great respect for people who honestly achieved success". Within less than two weeks, I've managed to deal with both negative patterns.

My income jumped about 30% up, and I've gained inspiration for dozens of articles, and 4 more new e-books I will write this year. That's for first affirmation. For second one, here's an example. My friend, Courtney, have published an article in latest TAPS Paramagazine issue. Normally, I would envy her, and even feel sad because she did it, and I didn't. But honestly, when I've learned about her success, I was so happy as it would be me whose got published . An awesome change of point of view!

You see how affirmations work. Earlier, I have said that affirmations might work after few days, weeks or even months. Indeed, there's no set-in-stone time for affirmations, because some negative patterns in your mind are weaker than others, and some are more established than others. Weak patterns can be dealt within few weeks, and difficult, and established patterns might require few months to overwrite. How to know when affirmation starts working? To understand this, you need to learn how to write and use affirmations.

How To Write And Use Affirmations

Before I explain how to write affirmations, I want to say that there are other methods of using affirmations, as well. You can record them and listen to them with your mp3 player; you can speak them aloud few times a day; you can paint them; you can type them on a computer, but based on experience of many people you should know that these methods require a lot more time for affirmation to work. The best way to my opinion is hand-writing.

Therefore, you need a notebook. You shouldn't use the same notebook that you're using as your psychic journal. Use a new, fresh notebook, devote it solely for the purpose of affirmations. When you open it, you can write your affirmations on the left page. On the right page, you should write all your responses. What is a response in case of affirmations? When you write an affirmation, you get a response from your body – it's either physical response or emotional or mental one. For example, you might:

Feel physical pain, recall past memories, feel emotional pain, or fear, or get any kind of emotion – positive or negative. You might even have positive physical responses, like pleasure, or you can get simple thoughts like "this is not real", "this is stupid", "fake" or positive thoughts like "awesome", "yea, it's true". All these responses should be written down with no judgment - just write them, and don't judge yourself because you have some negative thoughts. If you focus on them, you get angry or scared, and this only makes things worse.

The point is to write all these responses on the right page, so they won't be stuck in your subconscious anymore. An affirmation starts working when you get only positive responses from your body and mind, it means when you write your affirmations, you get only positive sensations, thoughts and emotions, with no negative responses. This might take weeks or even months.

Some schools of thoughts say that you should write affirmations for 30 days, or even for 90 days. Well, my school of thought is different. You should write down affirmation for 7 days at least – if after 7 days you still got negative responses, then continue writing your affirmations until you will get positive responses only – this is the only rule you should stick to when it comes to answering the question "how long should I write". Personally, today I write affirmations for no less than 21 days – but usually, I expand this period to 30, or even 40 days.

Now how to write affirmations, any way? You already know they should be as positive as possible. But you can't just write "I'm happy", because the way we perceive ourselves is not just ours. I mean, the way you see yourself is shaped by your thoughts and their thoughts – opinions and gossips of other people. Therefore, you should write down each affirmation in three persons, like this:

> *I, Nathan, make money simple and with pleasure.*
> *You, Nathan, make money simple and with pleasure.*
> *He, Nathan, makes money simple and with pleasure.*

And this set of affirmations should be repeated 5 times, so in total, you will write 15 phrases. If you're dealing with difficult pattern, you can also write 30 phrases or even more, if you like. As you can see, writing affirmations is quite simple.

Working With Affirmations

When you write affirmations, please don't act like a machine – feel enjoyment when you write each word, use your heart and "love" the phrases you're writing. By adding positive emotions to positive affirmations you're improving their effects, they just work better. But if you will write things down automatically, just to write them, then they won't really work as they should be. So, feel positive!

I need to mention a very important thing – after few days, or perhaps weeks of writing your affirmations, you might experience a mental breakdown. You may get sad, angry, and you may think this doesn't work. Do not stop writing affirmations now – because such a breakdown is a sign that affirmation is beginning to overwrite your old patterns! You must be strong, because few days later negativity will be gone, and your affirmation will really start to work. Some people experience these breakdowns, and some don't. But if you're going to experience it, remember to keep writing affirmations, as breakdown is a good sign.

Affirmations For Inner Growth And Psychic Development

Because affirmations are tools for working with your subconscious, they can be used for your inner growth. You can use them to deal with negative thought patterns that we all have, and overwrite them, change negative thoughts into positive thoughts. But they can be also used for psychic development. How?

Remember what I've told you about my financial problems earlier? Now think about it – what do you think about psychics? Do you respect people who can see auras, spirits, who can do psychic readings? Do you respect people who make money because of their psychic abilities, or with the help of these skills? If your answers are "no", then explain – how do you intend to become a psychic, if you don't respect psychics? Whether you like it or not, but your subconscious will simple block your efforts.

Or let's say you have been taught that all psychics are frauds faking stuff, and psychic abilities don't exist. Right now you might think "I want to learn how to be psychic", but because your subconscious beliefs are blocking you, you will be constantly hitting the wall, and you won't achieve much. Or perhaps you're afraid of what people will think of you if you will become psychic. In such case, your subconscious will again block you from learning psychic skills.

In such cases, you have negative patterns in your mind, and you need to deal with them – affirmations are a good way to do so. You can write "I, NAME, have respect for every psychic", "I, NAME, have respect for every psychic who makes money with the help of psychic abilities", "I, NAME, allow people to respect me because of my psychic abilities", "I, NAME, know that psychic abilities are real" and so on. Yes, working with such affirmations might take months – but trust me, if you won't start working with them today, and subconscious blockages do exist in your case, then your practice efforts might be worthless.

Affirmations can be used for many things – to reprogram negative patterns that govern different areas of your life: money, relationship, psychic development, spiritual growth, hobby, job. 20 minutes of writing per day are not much, but it can change your life – sometimes within weeks, sometimes within months, but in the end, your effort is really worth it.

Emotional Healing Work

Now we can move to more effective method of dealing with your blockages. Cleansing your subconscious, thus also removing energy body blockages can be performed through many different techniques, like affirmations, which you already know. Personally, I use a technique which I call "Emotional Healing Work". This technique is based on teachings of Robert Bruce, with some modifications made by myself. The essence of the technique is called "core images", and the overall core images work has been mixed by me with Silva's method, and auto-programming meditation. This technique can help you deal with negative past memories and experiences very fast and easy. As you should already know, dealing with your past is an important step in psychic development and personal growth.

The Problem Lies In Blockages

Every bad memory or experience or negative pattern creates blockages on energy channels (meridians) or chakras, thus the energy cannot flow freely, and thus, your chakras cannot return to a proper balance.

This always results in problems with psychic abilities – either you cannot develop your psychic sensitivity, or you can't hear your intuition, or no psychic abilities works for you. Some people don't have this problem, as their blockages are minor. But some people got huge blockages that block their psychic development path for good. But not only that. Subconscious blockages can also block your efforts to run a successful business, or have a successful relationship, or achieve your personal goals or dreams.

This is why it's important to deal with your subconscious blockages – not only to improve your overall psychic abilities, but also to improve your life and make few steps on the path of personal growth. You already know a great technique to deal with your problems – affirmations. But affirmations can be a slow tool. Core images, on the other hand, are very, very fast, because they hit the source of your problems directly.

I need to post a disclaimer here. Not everyone will benefit from Emotional Healing Work. Everyone is different, and some people might have troubles with breathing, relaxation, visualization, and so on. Some people might have other blockage that makes it impossible to use core images work. How so? For example, you might have been taught that such "mind programming" is just a trick, and it doesn't really work. In such case, emotional healing won't work because of your belief. Therefore, you will have to write down affirmation to remove that blockage, in order to start working with core images later.

Still, try it anyway – because there's no way of knowing if this technique works for you if you won't try it.

Healing Your Emotions

What do you need to start working with core images? Well, at least these things: some free time, peace and quiet, dark room or something to cover your eyes, because darkness improves your relaxation. And of course, you need to relax on a comfortable chair or bad. Finally, you need core images to work.

Preparing The List Of Core Images

The term "core images" refer to all negative patterns (beliefs, opinions), memories and experiences you have. These images not only create blockages, but often they can also act as attachment points for astral entities and psychic vampires, and it's a good idea to remove them in order to get rid of vampiric attachments and astral beings that feed on you. In order to work with core images, you need to be aware of them, and you need to create a list of them.

Therefore, prepare a notebook, in which you're going to write down your images. This can be the same notebook that you're using as your psychic journal, or it can be completely different notebook. When your notebook is ready, you need to start identifying your core images.

- When you write down affirmations, on the right page of your notebook write down your emotional responses. Sometimes, you might recall a bad memory or belief like "*no, no, life is difficult*". Your bad memory is the core image to work with, and your belief is a message that someone taught you, that life is difficult, and you have to recall the memory of that "lesson".
- When you do something, and suddenly you recall some memory that brings emotional charge with it that is negative charge like sadness, aggression, depression, fear, then this memory is a core image.
- Any negative memory you have creates core images to work with. If someone punched you when you were a child, then it's a core image. When you lost your favorite toy as a child, it's a core image. When your boyfriend broke up with you, and he brought emotional pain, it's a core image. This creates negative belief patterns: beating might have created a belief that people

are only waiting to punch you; loosing your toy might result in fear of losing in the future; heartbreak of teenager will create relationship problems in the future.
- Any negative pattern you have can be traced back to negative memory and experience. Just observing your behavior is a good way to identify your core images. Ask yourself why do you behave this way? For example, imagine that you've met that nice lady, she's kind, good-looking and intelligent, but you're afraid to talk to her. Ask yourself, "why am I afraid to talk with her", and during core images work session, try to recall your very first memory when you had problem talking to a girl (you will learn how to recall memories in just few moments) – et voila, you got your core image.
- **Observe your dreams** – keeping dreams journal is always good thing to do, and dreams can also carry information about core images for you. Observe your dreams and pay attention if there are any experiences from the past that might occur to you in a dream state. Write them down, even if they're not true memories, but typical dreams – work with dreams then, as they might also help you remove some blockages and negative patterns.
- **Sometimes, different events in your life might trigger negative memories** – buying a new car, meeting a new person, getting a new job etc. Pay attention to all memories and emotions that are coming to you each day.

Continue the work on your core images list – it might contain few points, or few hundred points, it doesn't really matter. A word of advice – do not worry if you have hundreds of things to work with. Work with them point by point and be patient. Worrying will only generate new core images to work with in the future. Think about big lists in a positive manner. Think, that now you know what you need to deal with. Think that with this big list you have, you will soon deal with all your problems and your life will change within few months.

Emotional Healing Work Session

Now you have your list of core images, it's time to have your first work session. So find some time to relax in quiet, dark place, or use something to cover your eyes. Darkness will help you relax. Sit down or lie in a comfortable position. Remember first few points from your list – one, two, maybe even five. Don't push yourself, five images per session are enough. Personally, I'm working with a maximum of three core images per session.

Now, follow the procedure carefully. Be sure no one will disturb your peace for the next half an hour.

1. You have to close your eyes, and relax all your muscles. Now you have to start breathing – take deep breaths. Breath in and breath out fast, one second to breath in, and one second to breath out. Make from three to ten of such breaths, no more. And then, again – relax.
2. Say "I'm going back with my memory to…" and define the moment of time, the moment when your experience has been recorded and is now a memory. Then observe that entire experience once more. Negative emotions might appear, just observe them. They're no longer in control, so don't be afraid, don't worry. You might want to cry – that's OK, cry. It's an emotional response meant to decrease emotional pain.

3. Observe the event you've just recalled. Relax, don't worry, don't be afraid, just observe it. Say "I'm observing, and I'm feeling good, I'm relaxed, I'm calm, I'm secured" and feel good, feel relaxed, feel calm, feel secured. You're in control. Know, that what you're observing is the past, and that past cannot hurt you anymore from your current point of view. You're safe.
4. Say "When I count down from 3 to 0, my fear/sadness/anger/depression will go away, and I will feel good, relaxed, calm and secured". Then slowly count down from 3 to 0, and let go all your negative emotions. Feel good, relaxed, calm and secured.
5. Often, some memories might carry additional belief – that you're responsible for something, or that someone is responsible for something. For example, when you have made a huge mistake, you might think it's all your fault. Or that when someone broke your heart, its that person's fault. In such case, forgive yourself or that person. Just say "I'm forgiving myself ..." or "I'm forgiving NAME ...", and when forgiving, do this with your heart – really forgive yourself or that specific person. It will be a relief for both of you.
6. Now visualize a beautiful scene – visualize a place you enjoy. For example, I'm visualizing wonderful plains with high grass, calm and warm wind, at the time of sunset. You need to visualize a scene you enjoy, it might a romantic sunset, or peaceful Buddhist's temple, or whatever. The point is that this visualized place must feel safe to you. You must feel at peace when looking at this place, you must feel calm, relaxed and secured. Use your vivid imagination!
7. Now visualize the scene, the event or experience in question, visualize it as paper postcard. This postcard is

hovering within your peaceful scene which you have visualized in the previous step. Then visualize that postcard moving away, and away, and away, until it disappears beyond the horizon.
8. Now visualize the postcard back again, it's hovering in front of you, within your peaceful scene. Visualize that you're holding a blessed sword in your right hand, and holy flaming torch in your left hand. Use the sword to cut the postcard to pieces. And then use the torch to burn these pieces. Visualize the pieces to burn entirely, leaving no trail, and see that beautiful, peaceful scene you've created earlier. Focus on it's beauty, and all the positive emotions the scene brings you. Enjoy it as long as you want.
9. Say "Thank you that I'm now free" and that's all – you can now open your eyes and end your session, or move to another core images and repeat steps 2-7.

It might look complex, but after few sessions, you will learn. Each session might take as little as 5 minutes, or even 30 minutes. Personally, I never needed any longer session, and I don't advice you to push yourself to the limits. After 30 minutes, end your session. If there are still emotions attached to your core images, just mark that on your list. You will return to this core image next time. Don't push yourself!

How To Recall Memories

In addition, if you've identified negative pattern, but not the core image itself, you might want to use a simple method of recalling bad memory.

1. You have to close your eyes, and relax all your muscles. Now you have to start breathing – take deep

breaths. Breath in and breath out fast, one second to breath in, and one second to breath out. Make from three to ten of such breaths, no more. And then, again – relax.
2. Say "When I will count down from 3 to 0, I will return with my memory to the first time when ..." and name the pattern you're working with, for example, "... when I was afraid to speak with a girl". Your mind should respond with a memory – it might not be the memory you were seeking, but still, it's a core image of some sort, somehow related to the pattern you're working with. Use it!
3. In the case when you won't get any memory, don't worry. After working with some images, you will deal with many blockages, and new images will appear to you. It takes time to fix your subconscious, but it's worth it!

Additional Tips For Working With Core Images

Below are some additional tips for working with core images.

- As I said, sometimes you might end your session, and you won't feel relief. On the contrary, you might feel that the core image is not yet cleansed. In that case, don't worry. Some powerful emotions require more time to deal with than weaker emotions. Just return to the specific image during the next session. Use as many sessions to deal with specific image as you need. Remember – you're not a contest, don't rush, be patient and take your time.

- Core images can be old or very fresh. Work with both types. If you had an argument yesterday, then it's core image, and it need to be cleansed as soon as possible. Treat it as any other core image.

Regarding that fresh images, I have a story for you from my personal practice:

Few days ago I had minor blockage on my subconscious – I was lead by fear, sadness and anger because my boss didn't pay me this month. These emotions were primary emotions I had, and for some reasons it influenced all my additional income. So I decided to use Core Images and cleanse these fresh emotions that appeared few days earlier.

I cleansed the negative emotions, and freed myself from them, then took a nap. After waking up and checking my email, I was surprised learning that I just made a record of daily passive income by selling so many copies of my books.

Some might say it's coincidence, but I'm psychic long enough to understand that coincidences are psychic phenomena as well, and they're not accidental, they're intentional.

Finally, you might ask "I'm done with the core image – should I feel anything?" – well, you might feel a relief. Or you might even sense more energies flowing through specific part of your body if you're psychic sensitive enough. Or you might notice changes in your daily life. The only thing you should really feel is nothing.

I'll explain – that nothing refers to your emotions when consciously recalling specific core image. That's why you should not destroy your images list. Read it from time to time once again, and recall the events and memories. If you can feel negative emotions, then it means the core image hasn't been cleansed yet, and you still need to work with it. But if you're recalling the event or memory, and you can't feel negative emotions at all, then it means you've successfully dealt with the image and you should be proud.

Everything else, like physical sensations or life changes, is just the result of your work. But – there's an important thing I need to say. Sometimes, removing blockages might result in serious physical response – you might catch the flu, or you might notice a pimple on your face (and it doesn't matter you're 60 years old), or you might get muscle spasm or like that. Don't worry, this is a good sign, it means that your energy body is working to heal itself. You should see my face today after I dealt with some nasty attachments.

Working With Positive Images

There's one more thing I need to mention – positive core images. These are the images usually related to astral entities and psychic vampires. They're like open doors for these beings, allowing them to attach to you and feed upon your energies. These images can be cleansed as well, but with little different approach.

In case of positive images, you feel positive emotions – if the image is allowing an entity to feed upon you, it needs to be cleansed. You can dot his with standard procedure, with a small difference to points 3 and 4. Instead of saying that you "feel good, relaxed, calm, secured", say and feel that you're neutral and calm, and that positive emotions are leaving. Say "*I'm no longer accepting these emotions, I'm no longer allowing access, I'm closed to these entities*". The point is to change positive emotions into neutral emotions – not negative, but neutral. Your subconscious must know that you're closed for anything that might be attached to these specific core images.

After few weeks of working with core images, you might notice a difference. Your approach to life might be more positive, and your psychic sensitivity might increase, while your psychic abilities might begin to awake, etc. But it doesn't matter why do you want to work with the core images. You might want to increase your psychic abilities or to get out of debt. In any case, the effort of your work is worth it.

Working with your mind is probably the most important step in psychic development. As the quote at the beginning of this chapter states, "to the mind that is still, the whole universe surrenders".

Safe Psychic

"Those who seek the easy way, do not seek the true way."

Before we move further, you should learn a bit about safety rules of psychic development. There are few things you should keep in mind. First of all, remember to take things gently. Do not rush, and try to follow the schedule of this book. Sure, it might take from half a year, to a whole year of training, before you can notice any results, but I'm not willing to provide you with 7-days psychic development course only to get you possessed. Or killed. No, seriously, there is no such thing as 7-days psychic development course. Within seven days, you might learn a bit of theory. But you won't become psychic, this, my friend, takes many months. But it also guarantees that you will become psychic, and not a victim of wrong practices.

Shopping Centers Are Evil

Well, not really, but shopping centers, supermarkets, concerts, stadiums, or even esoteric fairs, aren't the best place to spend your time. At least not when you will start to develop your psychic abilities. Such places often contain a lot of negative energies that can distract your energy system, or cause blockages, or cause something as simple as headache or flu. Try to spend as little time in places of high concentration of highly emotional people as possible. Remember to ground yourself, and set psychic shield.

Once, I spend few hours in a small café in Wroclaw. You should sense the energies there. Half an hour have passed, and I was suffering from a headache already. The entire place was (and probably still is) filled with negative energies of negative people. Know this, negative places attract negative people – it's law of attraction. If you will ever decide to run a spiritual restaurant or café, and you will apply the rules of Feng Shui, place some energetic paintings, and cleanse the place from time to time, then do not be surprised if you won't get many customers. In such case, invest in good promotion, to attract spiritual workers. As normal people will simple stay away from your place. It's because they're not attracted to it. Even more, they are repelled from it because they all think with negative patterns. The same patterns you're working to get rid of.

Ghosts And Spirits

In your psychic work, you might encounter ghosts and spirits, and other entities, as well. If you haven't been working with these entities before, and you don't have a teacher to guide you in this field, then please, do not work with these beings. Seek someone who can perform spirit releasement, as you're not the right person to do this when you have no experience. Spirits can form attachments similar to vampiric attack, and it's not pleasant.

In most cases, try to stay away from haunted places, and places of bad reputation. You can find many nasty entities there seeking people to feed upon. And until you will deal with most of your blockages, you're an easy target. On the other hand, don't get too paranoid. Just relax, not every spirit is dangerous. To be honest, rarely any spirit is dangerous. Just stick to the rules – avoid haunted places, and negative places, as well.

After few months of psychic development, when you've worked out few dozens of serious blockages, and you know how to create a psychic shield, if you want to deal with paranormal investigations, go for it! But before you do, learn a bit about prayer and meditation in the next chapter.

Your Sacred Space

In addition, you should remember to keep your house clean and ready for spiritual work. Or at least your flat. Or a room. How to do this? First, no clutter. Dirty room means dirty energies, and bad energies aren't good for psychic development. You should clean your room at least once a month, both physically, and energetically. To cleanse the room of negative energies, you can smudge the room with incense smoke, and light a candle for few hours. You can also place some energetic paintings on the wall, or follow the basic rules of Feng Shui.

When you perform psychic reading or energy healing of some sort, remember to cleanse the room of negative energies first. This also applies to distant readings, in such case, your 'customer' should at least light a candle. Candle flame is very universal in general. During each of your psychic or spiritual exercises, and works, remember to have a candle flame burning. It is known to burn negative psychic energies, and keep the room safe of any negative influence.

Use Your Intuition & Cleanse Yourself

Finally, use your intuition. When you sense that something is not right, or that something might be dangerous, then trust your instinct. With these simple rules, you will have much safer psychic growth, than without them.

Also, after each work with "customer", whether a friend or family member, or real customer, remember to cleanse yourself. Take a shower, and intend the water to cleanse you from negative energies. Meditate for few minutes, or smudge yourself with incense smoke, or burning candle flame. Especially, wash your hands with the intend to cleanse energies after each energy work session. This includes distant psychic work, as well.

As for incenses, one more important thing – always use natural incenses. Ask your incenses seller if the incense you're using is really natural. Artificial incenses aren't the best way to cleanse the room or yourself.

Breathe & Attraction

"Breath is Life"

Every psychic, through various means, will admit that breathe is essential to psychic growth. Through breathe, we collect psychic energies – Chi – to fuel both our normal life, and our psychic abilities, as well. Oxygen is life; breathing is life; breathing is Chi – life energy. The more you breathe, the better you breathe, the more energy you collect that can help your chakras grow, and your psychic abilities to function. When you start practicing breathing techniques, more energy will cause more negative patterns to re-emerge from your subconscious mind, so you will have more things to work with.

The more your breath, the better your energy flow is, and the more energy you have, the faster your psychic development is, and more psychic abilities you awake. Start practicing breathing techniques only when you will work out all the negative patterns you have identified without energy work or breathing technique. Do not speed things up. So, when your list of core images is empty, and everything has been worked out, start practicing breathing exercises. They will help you collect more psychic energies, and re-emerge more patterns to work with.

This is the part many psychic guides like books or teachers miss. Sometimes I think that it is because telling people that breathing and generally psychic development will cause life troubles, might scare people away. Well, no one ever said that growth is easy. But the benefits are worth the trouble. Without learning affirmations, meditation and emotional healing, you should not practice Tai Chi Chuan; or Yoga; or any other practice that merge breathing and energy work together. But because you already know the techniques to work with your mind, you can learn how to breathe.

Breathe With Your Diaphragm

Very first, and most important thing you need to know is that you should breathe with your diaphragm. It's that big muscle above your stomach (or in front of it, depends on your perspective), below your lungs. It's responsible for your entire breathing process. Western civilization teaches to breathe with your upper body, while this breath is incomplete. When you go to Yoga or Tai Chi Chuan classes, they will teach you that you need to breathe with your diaphragm, so your breath is full and complete.

How to breathe with your diaphragm? Lie down on the ground or bed, and start breathing. Notice that your diaphragm is moving, while your upper body does not. Now get up, and inhale, using your diaphragm – take a deep breath, then exhale, using your diaphragm only, without your upper body intentional movement. That's all. You're pushing your diaphragm outward when breathing in, and you're pulling your diaphragm inward, when breathing out.

If you have been taught to breathe in a wrong way, it might take months to learn correct breathing with your diaphragm. Don't worry about this, though, just practice Zazen meditation, and then Throat Chakra Breathing which I'm going to teach you in just few minutes, and with time, your subconscious will learn a new way of breathing, that will become your new habit.

Throat Chakra Breathing

You will now learn how to breathe with your Throat Chakra. Breathing through this chakra leads to chakra's development, and this chakra is important as it allows energies to flow into upper chakras, thus improving your intuition and general psychic abilities. After working for a while with this form of breathe, you might notice your psychic intuition kicking in. But don't think about this now, focus on learning to breathe.

This exercise requires two crystals. You can use pure quartz crystals, and they will do just fine. Pick up the crystals, one per hand, and then, extend your hands on the both sides of your body, palms should face top. Open your fists, and let the crystals just lie down. Place your foots on the ground or floor, and start breathing.

Inhale while facing forward. Then turn your head to the right arm, and exhale, saying "hooo". Then inhale again, while turning your head forward. Exhale again, while turning your head to your right arm again. Make at least four of such inhales.

Then inhale while turning your head forward. Exhale, saying "huuu", while turning your head to your left arm. Make at least four of such inhales.

Finally, continue the process for at least 6 minutes, four inhales and exhales per each arm.

Continue this exercise for another month. During the time of performing this exercise, you might witness many subconscious blockages re-emerging, only to be added to your core images list, and then deal with. After a month, you might either stop the exercise, and move to other practices, or perform the exercise from time to time, especially when outside, facing nature. It's a great technique of collecting additional amount of Chi.

Heng Haa Breath

You will now learn how to perform Heng Haa breat. It's a breathing technique often practiced by practitioners of Tai Chi Chuan and Chi Kung (Qi Gong), and I have a positive experience with the technique. When I started to breathe this way for the first time. I was jogging at the time for 30 minutes per day, and it was the maximum of my abilities. After two days of practicing Heng Haa, I managed to jog for an entire hour, and after that, my daily jogging sessions jumped from 30 to 45 minutes per day. I simple begun to collect more life energies, that I was able to use for my stamina.

The breath itself is very, very simple. Sit down, and breathe normally. Inhale deeply, and relax. Push your diaphragm outward as much as possible, inhale as much air as possible. Then say "haa" aloud and then exhale, pull your diaphragm inwards as much as possible. Extend the sound "haa" until you have exhaled nearly all the air from your lungs. Then shout, with the rest of the air, the word "heng", make a short pause (little less than one second), and once again, inhale by pushing your diaphragm outwards. Then repeat the entire process.

Practice Heng Haa each day. For the first week, breathe this way for 2 minutes. During the second week, practice Heng Haa for 3 minutes. Next week is Heng Haa for 4 minutes, and finally, during the forth week, you will be breathing for 5 minutes. From that moment on, you should practice Heng Haa each day, or at least few times a week.

A Matter Of Inner Growth

At this point, you should notice more and more core images being written down by you in your notebook. But it's not mandatory. Do not expect that when you will start breathe exercises, or that when you will start your energy work, then all your negative patterns will re-emerge. It varies from person to person. Some people will have to work with one core image each day, some people will have one core image to deal with each few months. Sometimes you might think there are no new core images, and you might be right. Some images might re-emerge after months or years of practice. But after all, it's not some kind of huge mess.

There will be dark days, and weeks of happiness, weeks of work, and months of enjoyment. Consider your inner grow as your biggest life adventure – when devoted to working on yourself, you can achieve things most people don't even dream about.

Sure, sometimes it can be difficult. But with time and patience, and work, you will work out your core images. It's not very hard and very problematic, this emotional healing. As always, there are better and worse moments. But in the end, the benefits are worth it, as I used to say many times. Remember – every experience is a learning experience. Do not run from your problems, face them! Only then, when you will be ready to work with your mind, you will be on the right path. Again, the answers you seek, lies within.

Psychic Shaping Life

For now, you should have enough things to work with – core images, affirmations, breathe exercises and such. Because of this, I will give you a small break. Continue your work, but before moving to energy work, and psychic techniques, I will teach you about the law of attraction, synchronicity, and ways to shape your life. After all, psychic mind is a tool that can turn your life upside down, and it can make your life just awesome. Being psychic is not just about inner growth, helping people, doing psychic readings and such. It's also about living the life you want.

Of course, if I would discuss the law of attraction and how to use this law in shaping your overall life, I would have to write an entire book about it (which, by the way, I plan to write). For the purpose of this book, I'm going to explain the basic rules that apply to the law of attraction when it comes to using it for psychic development. While you can't summon an ability to yourself, you can definitely summon answers, books, tips and people that can help you learn some cool psychic stuff.

Synchronicity & Coincidences

After spending few months on working with your mind, you might start to notice strange coincidences. For example, you might think about a specific car, and within next few minutes, you might spot that specific car on the street. Or you might think about an old friend whom you haven't seen in years, and then that friend might call you. Or you might want something to happen, because it would help you, and that thing you wished, really happens. Such coincidences fall into a category of synchronicity. In simple terms - coincidences aren't coincidences, they're elements of psychic phenomena. So, when some skeptic will tell you "this is just a coincidence", then admit it - and smile, because he just confirmed your psychic experience. In reality, coincidences are psychic experiences. Things happen because we think about them, or we think about things, because are happening now, or they will happen in the future.

The truth is that we are all connected. Living beings create one big living organism on planet Earth, one big network of minds and thoughts. Actions and thoughts of one person affect actions and thoughts of everyone else on this planet. Do you really think that you have stumbled upon this book by accident? Do you really think that you have met someone by accident? There are no accidents in the world - everything is a result of manifestation tool - your thought. And thoughts of everyone else on this planet.

Make a note in your journal

From now on, write down all the coincidences - when something happened, and you know you were thinking about it earlier, make a note about it in your journal. It will improve your psychic intuition, and they will also teach you about the way things are interconnected with everything else in this world.

Know this, everything that happens, happens for a reason. Every person you meet, every event, every experience, these things are meant for something. Every experience is a learning experience. Some things are meant to teach you something, some are meant to show you that you walk a wrong path. Pay attention to everything that is happening to you, and consider everything a lesson. Pay attention to these lessons. Every experience; book; person; word; phrase heard in the radio; people saw on TV, these are the reactions to our actions, both responses and answers we seek. When you want to know something, the answer will come to you. The answer might appear as message on TV, or music tune in the radio, or a phrase spoken by your friend.

I mention this, because you need to understand that by asking simple questions, you get simple answers. It's the way things work, it is the famous law of attraction – whatever you think about, turns to be reality. It doesn't apply only to attracting money, but it also applies to seeing answers, teachers, and things like that. Even this book, this very book is an answer to your actions and thoughts – maybe you wanted to learn how to develop psychic abilities, or maybe you wanted to learn if this stuff is real. These are obvious things, but there are thousands of books about psychic development on the market. Yet for some reasons, you decided to pick up this book. There's a lesson in this book meant for you – it might be the entire book, or it might be a single phrase somewhere in the middle, that might prove to be very, very inspirational for you.

For some reasons, you read this book. For some reasons, you have met that person. For some reasons, you have stuck in traffic; or stumbled upon that restaurant. Everything that happens, happens for a reason. It's that simple. This knowledge can be very useful. Because knowing that the Universe responds to your wishes, can improve your psychic development process.

The Basics Of The Law Of Attraction

The law of attraction is simple – you get what you think about. When you focus upon something, you attract it. And this rule applies to everything in this world. When you think you're rich, you attract money. When you think you're poor, you attract financial problems. When you think you're psychic, you're beginning to develop your abilities. When you think you're not psychic, then you're right, you can't learn psychic abilities. So the point of attracting the things you want is to think about the things you want, and ignore the things you don't want. It's that simple. And it's the same thing every single teacher of the law of attraction will tell you. But rarely, the teacher will mention the fact that your subconscious doesn't believe your wishes, then it won't attract the things you want. And even more than this, if your subconscious is filled with negative thoughts and patterns, it will attract them – it's because subconscious is connected to your astral body, and every manifestation takes place on the astral plane first.

Therefore, the point of really attracting the things you want is to get rid of negative patterns, that might attract negative things. In classic law of attraction, it is accomplished by pure belief – after months of believing that you can really attract something, you're re-writing the pattern in your subconscious mind. But you already know other methods of re-programming your mind – affirmations, emotional healing and meditation. The more you practice these things the greater number of negative patterns is gone. And you can replace them with positive beliefs, that can attract positive things.

Let me give you very simple example. Let's say you suffer from financial problems. But you're trying to attract money with the law of attraction, yet it doesn't work well, and you don't know why. So you search your memory, and you find a pattern, a lesson gave to you by your father when you were a child. Your father taught you that rich people are dishonest liars, and they have committed many crimes in order to get their money. If you believe this with your subconscious, then here's answer to your financial problems – you can't be rich, because your subconscious minds believe that rich people are bad people, and you don't want to be a bad person. Therefore, the way to deal with this problem is to delete this negative pattern, this negative belief, and then focus on making money. You will surely notice a difference.

The above is the simplest example of how mind patterns block the law of attraction. Basically, when you have negative beliefs about something, you will attract the negative things you're afraid of. And if you have positive beliefs, you will attract positive things. In order to shape your life, you need to get rid of bad patterns, and replace them with positive thoughts. This can be achieved through practice of affirmations and emotional healing. The less negativity is stored in you, the higher the vibrations you have. This results in better energetic flow, better chakras energetics, better psychic abilities, and easy to use law of attraction.

The Law Of Attraction And Psychic Pursuits

While the above knowledge can be applied to each and every aspect of your life, because of the subject of this book, I want to discuss the use of law of attraction and synchronicity in regards of psychic development. You already know that you might have negative patterns about psychic abilities, stored in your subconscious. So you need to get rid of it. If you believe that psychic abilities do not exist, then you will fail; if you think that it's only a gift from God that cannot be learned, you will fail; if you think that being a psychic is scary, then you will fail.

The best thing you can do right now is to collect a list of all your fears, and false beliefs about psychic abilities, and psychics themselves. Then use affirmations and emotional healing technique to heal these patterns, fears and beliefs. When you deal with them, you will be able to move on.

How to move on? When you believe that you can really learn psychic abilities and that psychic abilities are safe, you might have many questions and needs. For example, you might want to talk to a psychic teacher. Or you might need advices regarding some specific psychic exercise. Or you need any form of psychic help; or maybe you seek answers if the theoretical ability you think about is possible. So, you need to follow the simple rule – what you ask for, you receive. This is the law of attraction mixed with synchronicity. How can this 'ability' be unleashed? By simple asking the Source for guidance. When you seek a teacher, then just ask the Source (through prayer, or affirmation, or just a wish), "I would like to find a teacher of psychic development." And then, open your eyes, as within days, weeks, maybe months, the Universe will rebuild itself in such way that will allow you to find the teacher you seek.

Personally, I wanted to develop my psychic abilities further few years ago. At the time, I lived in a small village, and there was no teacher available there. But I made a wish – that I want to develop my psychic skills further. Then, coincidences started to happen. I went for a University to a big city of Wroclaw; then I have met a person on Twitter, and from that person, I have learned about her Open House meetings; I decided to create such meeting in Wroclaw; finally, on the first meeting I have met my teacher, who just shared a bit of his knowledge with the group; and thanks to his teachings, my abilities developed further. Don't expect that angels will knock at your door and will bless you with the answers. Expect inspirations, random thoughts, expect new people to appear in your life, new experiences and events. Small things, that lead to answer you seek.

If you seek advices, then ask for advices; if you seek help, ask for help; if you want to know if something is possible, ask if it's possible. And open your eyes and ears, waiting for answers. You might experience many synchronistic events – a song in a radio; a new person met in a bus; a new inspirational thought for a website; a random tweet on Twitter that can lead you to your small satori (illumination). Remember about one thing – you ask for something, and the Source answers. And it answers always. But sometimes, you just fail to see or hear the answer. So keep your eyes open – expect small coincidences to happen, instead of angels stomping ground. And have fun – because when you will learn what it's all about, then your life will start to change upside down.

Are you hungry for love? Ask the Source to point you for your love. Do you need money for psychic development workshop? Ask the Source about this money issue, and it will at least send you inspiration for making additional income. Or maybe you have problems at work? Ask the Source to help you out. And believe that the Source always answers your prayers – you just need to listen.

What Do You Focus Upon

As I said, you attract things you focus upon. So focus only on positive things. Instead of focusing on war, focus on peace and love. Do not focus on the dangers of nuclear power plants, focus on the beauty of creativity of people who design alternative, ecological technologies. Do not focus on evil spirits and demons that can possess you, focus on angels, the Source and loving, spiritual powers. Do not focus about bad things, focus only on the good stuff. Always look at the bright side of life – this saying never gets old.

Since your subconscious likes to collect a lot of useless information, I need to mention this: what kind of movies do you watch? What kind of music do you listen to? Unfortunately, a lot of people watch brutal and aggressive movies or listen to aggressive music. There's nothing wrong with AC/DC, but I really suggest you to stop watching movies that present brutal aggression, blood, murders, hate, suffering and pain. Also, you should stop listening to music that promote hate and aggression through the lyrics. And it doesn't matter if the song is in a language you don't understand. Your subconscious will understand. And it will work upon the patterns you feed it with. The more aggression and negative stuff you face in TV, cinema or radio, the more problems it generates. Simple as that.

New Age followers have this fancy term, a lightworker, it is a person that follow the light, think about positive things, do good things, help people, and use his skills and knowledge to change the world for better. Well, I wouldn't go that far, as I don't really like the New Age stuff, but you got the point. Be positive, be a good person, helpful to others. Try to make a change. And when you will be doing good things, the good things will be happening to you. It's the simplest way to describe the law of Karma. But don't worry about Karma – just be a good person. And take back the responsibility for your life, start shaping it the way you want. And enjoy!

New Energy Ways

"A jug fills drop by drop."

After few weeks, maybe even months of working with your core images, writing affirmations and meditating, you can start improving your overall energetics. As I already said, you can do this by practicing Yoga or Tai Chi Chuan, but if you don't have access to these methods, or if you want additional technique to work with psychic energies, you can learn New Energy Ways. The process of the energy body development should take about three months, but don't worry - this time will pass faster than you think. Pay attention, because energy body development is one of the most important steps described in this book, and this chapter explains more advanced techniques and methods of energy work you will need to use later to learn useful psychic abilities.

It's All About The Energy

Through years, it was a common practice to forget about energy work when developing psychic abilities. The truth is, without energy work no psychic ability is possible. Right now you're already familiar with such terms like energy body or chakras. The more you develop these two elements, the better and easier to use your psychic skills will become. Therefore, it is now time to move to one of the most important chapters of this book, the practical exercises meant to develop your energetics. After few months of working with New Energy Ways, you will not only re-emerge more subconscious patterns to work with, but you will also feel more energy in general. You will feel stronger; you will feel healthier; you will be more productive, and less stressed. It's the beauty of psychic energies, which are life energies, Chi.

Why Energy Body Is Required For Psychic Abilities To Work

What many psychic development guides tell to readers is almost useless without proper basics. Many psychics and energy workers write their guides based on personal experiences - I'm not exception of this rule. But the problem is that those psychics already have quite well developed energy body so all they have to do is to learn psychic techniques. Yet most of people who really want to develop psychic abilities do not have their energy bodies developed, and they have to work on their bodies first, then move to psychic techniques. Other books like this won't tell you this because, in most cases, authors themselves do not know about this simple fact. Of course, not every psychic development workbook forgets about energy work – but it's a common problem.

Yet even if I always had developed energy body, I was not aware of that - that's why I have started developing it. My training has not given me many results, and it led me to funny situations when I was disappointed of my own psychic development, I finally understood that I do not need to develop my energy body because it's already developed.

But this made me discover the simple fact that others do require to develop their energy body. Therefore, I put a whole section about this process within this book. But why do you need your energy body for using psychic abilities?

As I already said, energy body transfer psychic energies, it collects and utilities them. Only developed energy body can utilize these energies properly, and if they utilized as they should be, you can control them easily (as they "vibrate" with the frequency your own energy body vibrates), and you can access the information they carry (therefore, causing for example psychic reading to work). Rarely any other psychic development guide will mention this, but many guides will mention the importance of meditation – which is rising vibrations of the energy body. Meditation not only put mind at peace, but it also increase the frequency of the energies that flow through the energy system. And it rises this frequency just because your mind is quiet and operates on different brainwaves. All of this also connects to the fact that energy work also removes energetic blockages, that can cause psychic problems. In the end, energy work prepares your physical and etherical bodies for psychic work.

Energy Theory

Let's make a short review of knowledge gained in the previous chapters. Psychic development, beside working with your mind, is also about working with energies, so called 'psychic energies' - they're present around you all over the time. They're in every stone, in every person, they're inside of you, building your human energy body (bodies). They're in food, trees, animals. They carry information, interact with the physical world, and they can be negative, positive, or just neutral. They can be programmed to perform a specific task. They can be used by magical means, but as psychics, we stick with our mind only, and we do not use magical methods such as wands or rituals. These psychic energies are often called Chi, Prana; or they are marked with Greek letter PSI, introduced during psychic research, to mark the unknown factor that cause psychic skills to work. Some school of thoughts uses to differ elemental psychic energies from life energy, Chi, that is already utilized by energy body. But in reality, it's the same energy, just with different frequency, different vibration.

There are few things you need to know about psychic energies before you will learn how to manipulate them.

1. **Negative, positive, neutral** - some energies can be negative: they might cause aggression, sadness and other negative emotions. Other energies can be positive, causing happiness, and other might be just neutral, flowing around. You must be aware energies exist, and they can be found in different places. For example, haunted home will carry a lot of negative energies, while fresh green forest will carry positive energies, and the city will carry neutral energies. Be

careful where you're drawing energy, as it might be dangerous sometime.
2. **Overload and exhaustion** - your energy body have a limit of energies it can transfer a day. It's more complex than this, but it's what you must know right now. When beginning energy work, you must be careful not to draw too much energy at once, because it will overload your system. Vice versa, when you lack psychic energies, you might feel tired because you got used to larger amounts of these energies flowing through your body. Keep this in mind.

That's why we, psychics, are called "energy workers" — because we work with energy. There are also other energy workers, because once again it's a matter of terminology — real vampires or mages can be called energy workers, or even practitioners of eastern martial arts as well because these eastern systems work with Chi, as well.

A little bit of experimental theory — why there are negative, positive and neutral energies? Based on my personal observation, experiences and research made in my personal library, I came up with theory of psychic energy frequencies. In short, psychic energies vibrate in a scale of specific frequencies. Let's say the scale can be pictured as a ruler with twelve points. Points 0-4 will be negative, 5-8 neutral, and 9-12 positive. High vibration are positive energies, normal vibration neutral, and low vibration are negative. Now there's an interaction between all these three types of energies, for example, positive energies can pass their frequency to negative energies, generating more positivity. This is just a tip of an iceberg and a subject for another book, but I hope with this little piece of information I increased your interest in psychic energies.

Psychic healing systems like Reiki or Pranic Healing, or the system called "Healing Tao" also work with psychic energies, the Chi. Basically, the energy in use is always the same, the difference lies in techniques and terms. Some people say there are different types of energies, but it's just a problem of terminology, that's all.

Some people use the name of Chi and some use the Greek letter PSI. Well, PSI is a Greek letter indeed, yet I prefer to use it in order to mark the unknown factor when dealing with paranormal, and not to name the energy. There are also other names: Ether (aether), Prana, Odic force, Ki (or Qi). Hebrew tradition speaks of Ruach, the life force. And if have played any role playing game set in a fantasy world, then I'm sure you're familiar with a term 'mana'. Mana is a Hawaiian term. It doesn't matter which name you will decide to use, just remember that all these terms represent the same thing. For this book, we stick with the name of psychic or psychic energies, and from time to time I also use the term Chi.

Energy Body And Human Energy System

Energy body, as you already know, is one of the most important things when it comes to learning psychic abilities. This body is made of psychic energies in different states. It represents the human being on astral and etherical planes. We will not get into details regarding the astral plane in this book, because it is very wide subject. Basically, there are two planes that should interest you now – the physical plane, the one you can see right now with your eyes, and the astral plane, build of psychic energies (it is very general description, but you get the essence). For now, let's focus on the energy body.

As I said, the energy body is made of psychic energies flowing through channels - these energetic structures are called 'meridians' or 'nadises' (singular: meridian, nadis), and there are hundreds if not thousands of these. The channels look like physical veins, but I wouldn't look for any energetic walls, really. In reality, it's more like some unknown force holding the energies on their routes, creating streams of psychic energies – these streams are the energy channels.

These channels exist through the entire physical body, connecting energy centers - and there are three levels of these centers. Bigger ones are called 'Chakras', and there are seven of them. The name "Chakra" originates from Hindu beliefs and was brought to Western world through the teachings of Theosophy. They are located in the main body, vertically along the spine. First is located near the base of the spine, second in the abdomen, third in solar plexus, fourth near heart, fifth near throat, sixth between eyes, and seventh on the top of the head. Medium centers are just called medium centers, and they're located on joints. Smaller centers, so called 'energy exchange ports' or just 'ports' are located all over the body, and there are many thousands of these - they're responsible for exchanging the energy between body and surrounding area. Below is a short list of most important elements you need to keep in mind. In short, the energy body is made of:

- **Seven Primary Energy centers** - also known as Chakras, they're responsible for utilizing and distributing the energy throughout energy body. I will discuss them later in this book.
- **Two Medium Energy Centers within shoulders** - large energy centers within shoulders.
- **Two Medium Energy Centers within hips** - large energy centers within hips.
- **Energy Exchange ports** - located on whole skin, there are hundreds of thousands of these ports. They're meant to draw and release psychic energies.

- **Energy Channels** - they transport energies throughout energy body
- **Primary Energy Channel** - it goes along with spine, it draws Earth energy from the ground, and it acquires Cosmic energy from space.

You might have noticed that I speak of the energy body as connected to the physical body - yes. It is connected through unknown means to the nervous system, and that is why we can literally perceive physical or emotional illness on aura. Energy body generates energy field, the so called 'aura' - the energy field might range from few centimeters to about three meters outside the physical body and theoretically it can be perceived with "eyes" - at least this is what aura viewers says. Seeing energy is a lot more difficult thing to do and not a subject for beginners, instead of trying to see energies, let's focus on sensing and manipulating them first. But if you're eager to learn aura view, then I will surely discuss it later.

New Energy Ways - Developing Energy System

In this chapter, I will focus on explaining to you the New Energy Ways – a method of tactile energy manipulation which, in my eyes, is the best way to learn energy manipulation, and develop your whole energy system currently available, which you can practice in home with no teacher supervision. I will teach you exercises, methods of manipulating the energy, and I'll also present a universal schedule for you to stick with during your development.

A lot of psychic practitioners forgets about being patient. Many people would like to see results of their psychic development within days, even hours. This is impossible, even if you could create a psiball for the first time on the long run it won't make a difference because your body will not be able to sustain the amount of energies required by your psychic work. Because of this, paying attention to the following exercises is important. Take your time and keep in mind that 3 months of practice is nothing when compared to 50 years of your future psychic work. And let's get to practice, finally!

NEW And Tactile Manipulation

New Energy Ways is a method of energy manipulation developed by Robert Bruce. The system of energy manipulation is simple, and it's about literally feeling the energy moving through your energy system. It's easier than it sounds, because the whole manipulation is being accomplished by feeling the touch and movement on your physical body. From the previous part of this book you know that energy system is directly connected to the nervous system, so by stimulating nervous system you stimulate energy body and vice versa, by stimulating energy body you can also stimulate the nervous system.

To clarify, New Energy Ways should be understand as new ways of energy, not new energy, - which is a common misconception.

Developed energy body is required for almost all psychic work; therefore, in order to learn further about psychic abilities and development, for now you have to focus upon developing your energy system. How long will it take? It all depends on individual progress, but this book covers a simple three months schedule that should be enough for you to develop your energy body on the basic level that allows us to move forward.

During your energy system development, remember to continue your work with affirmations and emotional healing, Also, do not forget to meditate. There might be many negative patterns re-emerging during your energy work, so you need to be ready for them. The more you work with energy and core images, the better psychic you become.

The Energy System Is Like Car Engine

But first things first, you already know what energy body is. While psychic energies are like fuel, energy body is like an engine (and your mind in this metaphor will be the driver), it's build from different elements like energy centers and channels through which psychic energy flows. Some people have already developed energy body, which means their centers and channels are unplugged, and energy flows through them easily. Some people, like me, had to unplugged the channels consciously with New Energy Ways because the energy didn't flow as it should be through my system. This is what energy body development is - unplugging your channels and energy centers.

What you will learn from the next few pages is how to unplugged all your energy channels one by one, step by step. We will start from feet, through legs, arms and up to drawing energy into lower energy center, Lower Tan T'tien that will be known as LTT, and it's also known as Hara, or Hara region in Taoist schools of thought.

Introduction To New Energy Ways

There are few things you need to know before you start practicing NEW. First of all, there will be no visualization, because, in reality, most people can't visualize. They just think they can; therefore, all energy manipulation is based on tactile sensations. This brings us to a new term - Mobile Body Awareness (MBA). Your body's point of awareness is normally centered in the eyes because you perceive the world from this point day by day. Mobile body awareness is about changing your point of perception. In reality, it's a simple skill to learn, after few weeks of work you will find out you can do this naturally. Let's try some exercises.

Exercise 1: Focus totally on the thumb of your dominant hand. Feel its shape, size and position within the whole body. Just think about your thumb and nothing else. And that complete the exercise, you successfully moved the point of your awareness. This means you're ready for New Energy Ways. Try this exercise on different parts of your body, try to focus on your knee, your whole hand, or your big toe. Play around and keep it fun.

As you might have noticed, you didn't even need any deep level of focus, no trance or meditative state is required to practice energy work with NEW. All you need to do is to focus on your task. You need will to practice, as well, and finally, slightly relaxed body. But with time, you will be able to work with energy wherever you want, not matter the place or time or your emotional, psychical or physical state.

Exercise 2: You will now learn how to target your awareness. Let's get back to your thumb. Scratch it or rub it, feel the physical sensation and pay attention to it. This will help you focus on the specific part of your body, and whenever you'll have problems with moving your point of awareness, just use this technique of scratching or rubbing to focus.

Exercise 3: Now you're going to try something different. Move your awareness to your thumb in the right hand. Scratch it if you have to. Focus on the thumb for about 20 seconds then quickly move your awareness to the thumb of your left hand. Again, focus on it totally, feel the physicality of the thumb. After another 20 seconds, move your awareness to your left knee. Focus on it for 20 seconds, and then move your awareness to right knee and again focus totally on it. Pay attention to all the feelings and sensations you get. This exercise is meant to teach you how to move your point of awareness quickly around your body. Continue with the exercise, jumping between different areas of your body for another few minutes, then take a rest for 15 minutes, and continue again with few minutes session. Practice 3rd exercise for few days or so.

While practising above exercises, you might get physical sensations - warm, tingling, maybe even weird kind of pain. Don't worry, everything is OK, and in reality, all the physical symptoms are a good sign, they mean your energy system is responding to energy work. With time, physical sensations might disappear because the more developed the system is, the less physical response it gives. This happens because undeveloped energy system causes energy to push through channels and energy centers, and this might give physical sensations. If they energy doesn't push and it flows with easy, it means the channel or center is developed enough for the energy to have no problems with flowing.

Exercise 4: Now you're going to learn more advanced technique of tracing tactile sensations. Move your awareness to your right thumb again, but this time directly to the nail. Now start moving your awareness from the nail up to the area where the thumb connects with the wrist. Feel it like you would be moving your finger through your whole thumb. If you like, you can use the index finger of your other hand to touch the nail in your thumb, and while touching move it up to the wrist. Focus on the physical sensation and try to repeat it only with your mind using mobile body awareness. When you will reach the wrist, move back to the nail, and then again to the wrist and back. Continue with the exercise for about 3 to 5 minutes.

Try the above exercise with your other thumb and when you feel ready, try move the awareness from the thumb up your shoulder and back. For now, remember to move up and down, forward and back because you don't want to draw energy yet.

There will be time for this later. Continue with energy movement for another day or two.

Exercise 5: Try to move your body awareness to your both thumbs. This is called splitting. Within few months, it will be required to draw the energy through both arms and both legs. It is easier than it sounds, just focus on both thumbs at the very same time.

If you want, try all the exercises describe in this section with splitting your awareness, stimulate both thumbs and both knees at the same time. If you have trouble splitting awareness, however, please stick to working on one area or limb at a time until you feel more comfortable splitting awareness actions.

Exercise 6: Finally, focus on your right hand, then move your Mobile Body Awareness through your hand to your right shoulder, then through the neck to your left shoulder, down through hand to the left hand, and then go back to the right hand. Continue the exercise for 3 to 5 minutes.

All the six exercises described in this section are meant to introduce you to the New Energy Ways. Continue to exercise for few days until you feel you can move your body awareness easily throughout your entire body. If you have no problems with Mobile Body Awareness, you can move forward.

Make a note in your journal

How did you feel the energy? Was the above exercises difficult or not? Do you find any problems with manipulating psychic energies using NEW? Did you felt any pain, or was it quite pleasure sensations? Do you experience a problem with shifting your awareness? Have you noticed anything weird during the above exercises?

Awareness Hands

Now you know a little bit about practical energy manipulation, it's time to learn powerful technique that will make energy manipulation even easier. This technique is called awareness hands and it should be read literally - those are hands of your awareness. It cannot be easily explained, and you have you try it on your own. To do this, we will perform another exercise.

Exercise 7: You're going to draw energy forth and back through your right leg. Using tactile sensations imagine your right hand, palm to be specific, is scooping (drawing) the energy from the bottom of your feet up to your knee, then up to your hip and then back to your feet. Literally feel your palm moving forth and back throughout your leg and feel tactile sensations of the energy moving forth and back your hand, as well.

The point of this exercise is to learn how to sense your awareness hand moving through your leg. When you can feel it, (just like you performed all the earlier exercises) then I have to congratulate you, because you've learned another useful technique of energy manipulation. Now try to repeat exercise 7th, but this time use your both hands to move energy forth and back through both of your legs. It's simple awareness split, and you should have no problems with it.

Types Of Stimulation Techniques

There are few techniques called actions that are being used to stimulate energy body and all of them will be described now along with practical exercises that will help you learn each of them. Now you have to learn another term, the TI - Tactile Imagining. This is an extension of Mobile Body Awareness, and it includes specific techniques meant for energy manipulation.

- **Circling Action** - particularly used for stimulating energy centers located on joints (you should know that every joint is a place where medium energy center is located). This technique is based on making circles with your Tactile Imagining.

Exercise 8: Start making circles around biggest joint (the second joint in from the thumbnail) on your right thumb, around 1.5 cm in diameter, either clockwise or counter-clockwise, whatever works better for you. If you like, scratch the circular area around the joint to get a better focus and perspective. Use what you have learned and use the mobile body awareness to make circles around the joint for 3 to 5 minutes. Most people the physical sensations for the first time already, so don't be surprised if you will feel tingling, warm, pressure or something else. Try the exercise on your other thumb, as well. If you can't feel anything, just move to the next exercise. Stimulation will be successful another time.

The size of circles should be adapted to the size of the energy center. For example, energy centers within finger joints are small, while joints in your shoulders are definitely bigger; therefore, they require making bigger circles.

- **Brushing Action** - for stimulating energy channels, we are using straight, brushing move from one point to another through the skin, as we would be painting our skin with a brush. You've already try this kind of movement in exercise 4th.

Exercise 9: Focus on your thumbnail, and move your awareness back and forth to your wrist just like you were moving your finger back and forth touching the thumb. Continue with the exercise for 3 to 5 minutes. Once again, if you can't feel anything just move to the next exercise and don't worry, sensations will come eventually. Try brushing your whole hand, and your entire mind keeping in mind that you have to move the energy back and forth.

- **Wrapping Action** - this action is like moving your point of awareness around specific part of the body, as if wrapping an imaginary bandage around it over and over.

Exercise 10: Once again focus on your thumbnail, and move your awareness back and forth to your wrist just like before, but this time add a spinning move to the whole process, so your Mobile Body Awareness will be spinning back and forth around your thumbnail. Continue the exercise for another 3 to 5 minutes. Then, try spinning your Mobile Body Awareness around your whole hand or leg.

- **Tearing Action** - this action should be used mainly for primary energy centers (chakras) because those are probably the only points of your body this action is useful for. For this action, you have to use your Hands

of Awareness, and tear your energy center like tearing a calyx of a flower. For now, skip this action as there will be no practical exercise yet. It will be discussed later once we get to the point of opening chakras.
- **Sponging Action** - the final action is called "sponging" and it's what it seems to be - it's like drawing the energy with sponge through specific part of the body. This action will be used later for drawing the energy daily so pay attention.

Exercise 11: Use your Mobile Body Awareness and Hands of Awareness to move the energy within your thumbnail back and forth like you would be moving a sponge, sensing the energy inside your thumbnail. Continue for another 3 to 5 minutes. Try to split awareness into both thumbnails, or even whole hands.

That completes the set of actions. If you're not sure if you get them correctly, repeat all the exercises one more time. From my own experience, I can tell that if you think you understand these actions pretty well, you probably do.

Make a note in your journal
Can you use all NEW actions easily? Are there any actions harder to use than other?

How To Draw And Store The Energy

During first two months of the energy body development, you will cleanse your energy channels and develop energy centers, and your energy body will be prepared to store enough psychic energy needed for future psychic work. Therefore, you have to learn how to draw and store the energy.

As you already know, there are three energy storage centers - one in the abdomen, second near the heart and third inside your head. But for the purpose of drawing and storing the energy you will focus only on your first storage center, the Lower Tan T'ien (LTT). Do not draw the energy into your upper storage centers, it won't speed up your psychic development, more than that - it might damage your energy body and cause you many problems, both physical and mental in nature. Don't worry, these storage centers will be filled with energy, I will explain the process in just few minutes.

How To Draw The Energy

After two months of energy work, continue to draw energy with this technique below that will teach you how to draw the energy.

- Sit down in an arm chair or lie on a bed and relax. Make sure you feel comfortable. Again, no complex trance state is needed, just relax.
- First, warm up and use brushing action for 20 seconds on the fingers of both feet. Split your awareness if you can. Then use brushing action on the bottom of your feet for 20 seconds. Finally, use sponging action on both feet to draw the energy back and forth for 20 seconds. Your feet should be well warmed up by now.
- Clear your mind, and, by using your Hands of Awareness, or solely Mobile Point of Awareness, start drawing the energy from the bottom of your feet, through entire legs, into Lower Tan T'ien, which is located few centimeters below your stomach, about 4 to 6 centimeters inside your abdomen. Draw the energy

only one way, do not return it into the ground. Continue the process for 10 to 15 minutes.

And that's it - this is how drawing and storing the energy looks like. With time, the energy levels inside your Lower Tan T'ien will exceed the amount the LTT can handle, so the energy will be automatically transferred to the Middle Tan T'ien, and then higher, up to Upper Tan T'ien.

Energy Body Development - Schedule

Now you know how to perform different types of stimulation, and you are ready to start developing your energy body. Once started, you can stop at any time and start again from the point where you stopped your training. Energy Body development is probably the most time-consuming part of psychic development this book discuss. Therefore, don't worry - at first you might get inpatient but stick with the schedule. After a month, you won't have problems with practising, and after two months, whole practice will become a lot easier. Below are some additional tips for practising New Energy Ways.

- Practice for 5 days a week. Take weekends off and take a rest.
- The schedule isn't set in stone. If you believe you could take additional practice, just repeat the week.
- Sit down in a comfortable chair, or lie on a bed.
- When secondary energy centers or groups of exchange ports are found not to respond, continue on with the next exercise anyway, the energy centers will finally respond.
- Your eyes can be either closed or open, but for beginners, I recommend keeping them open.

- During first two months, practice for 45 minutes per day. During the last month, draw the energy for 15 minutes per day.
- Spend about 15-30 seconds on each type of movement/stimulation (action).

How to use this schedule? Let's take an example from the first week. For the big toes, you read "stir both main joints, then brush and wrap whole of each big toe". It means that you have to perform three exercises.

- First, you have to use stirring action on both main joints of each of your big toes.
- You need to use brushing action on both big toes.
- You need to use wrapping action on both big toes.

Each action should take about 15-30 seconds, and then you should move to another body part which is always marked with bold text. It's simple, isn't it?

And now, let's get to the actual schedule for three months of the energy body development.

Schedule

90 days, 45 minutes per day, then 15 minutes per day

Weeks	Body part	Actions description (20 seconds per action)
1-2 {45 min}	Feet	**Big toes** Stir both main joints then brush and wrap whole of each big toe.

		Lesser toes Brushing and sponging actions only used on each of these. **All toes** Wide brushing action across all toes on each foot. **Soles** Mobile rotary stirring action over entire surface of each sole. Wide brushing action on each sole. **Heels** Deep, wide stirring action on each heel. **Feet** Sponging action through whole of each foot.
3-4 {45 min}	Legs	**Ankles** Stirring action on inner and outer bony sides of both ankle joint. Wrapping action around each ankle. **Knees** Stirring, brushing, wrapping knees. **Legs**

		Brush each leg (4 pathways), from foot to hip, both directions. **Hips** Stir, then brush, each hip center (see cautions). Wrapping action around whole of each hip joint.
5-6 {45 min}	Hands	**Fingers** Stir thumb joints then brush and wrap each finger and thumb joint. Use wide brushing action across all fingers, side to side. **Hands** Wide brushing action along back of each hand, fingertips to wrists. **Palms** Rotary stirring action, then wide brushing action on each. **Hands** Use whole of hand sponging action, through both hands.
7-8 {45 min}	Arms	**Wrists** Stir inner and outer, then use brushing and wrapping action. **Elbows** Stir inner and outer, then use brushing and wrapping action.

		Shoulders Stir inner, outer, front, back, then brush & wrap. **Arms** Wide brushing action along outer, then inner, pathways. Sponging action through whole of each arm.
9-10 {15 min}	Legs	Draw energy into LTT through legs
11-12 {15 min}	Arms	Draw energy into LTT through arms

Energy Body Work After 3 Months

After 3 months of the energy body development, you will have to continue energy work daily. But after completing the schedule above your energy body development will focus on drawing energy into your Lower Tan T'ien - a process described in the exercise above that should take no more than 15 minutes each day. You can find details about the schedule at the end of this book.

Make a note in your journal
Keep notes of your development throughout all 3 months. Write down unusual experiences, bad and worse days, situations when energy manipulation is easier, or more difficult. Literally pay attention to everything and write everything down.

Summary

By continuing your practice, you are developing your energy body. You need to remember that this is one of the most important step in psychic development, so do not skip this chapter, please. With the energy system development, you can move further and open your chakras, and finally learn practical psychic techniques. Of course, if you want, then you can replace New Energy Ways with other energy manipulation system.

Psychic Arts

"Those who seek the easy way, do not seek the true way." - Lao Tsu

Hopefully (because I'm not sure if you haven't skipped the last section of this book, that wouldn't be good) you have developed your energy body, and you're drawing energy day by day for 15 minutes daily. It's time to learn a bit more about the energy system. First thing you need to learn is still related to your energy body. In order to perform safe energy work, three basic techniques must be learned - centering, grounding and filtering.

Psychic Field Maintenance

Psychic Field is, of course, a field of psychic energies gathered in a small area of space. But right now I will use the term to refer specifically to the psychic field surrounding human being - you. Energy Body and Aura together create energy field that extends from few centimeters to about two meters from your body. The closest parts of the etheric body are the... well, etheric body. Beyond that, one can perceive astral body, and finally mental body. This creates psychic field, a field that can be expanded consciously to create links or cover other people and objects. This will be used later for advanced psychic techniques. For now, you have to learn two new techniques - centering and grounding.

How To Center

Centering means finding your very essence. It relates to both mind and energy system, and even if this first sentence might sound weird, it reality it's very simple process. In order to center, close your eyes and focus on the very middle of your head (skull). Keep the focus there, and perceive the darkness in front of your eyes. With time, you will be able to center with opened eyes too, but for now practice with closed eyes.

And that's it - this is how process of centering looks like. As you can see, it's very simple; centering focuses your mind and balances your energies. It can be used before and after any form of psychic work, from energy manipulation to psychic readings and even psychokinesis, remote viewing or psychic healing.

In other form of centering technique, you don't focus on the middle of your head, but on your central energy channel within spine which you already know. The principles of this technique are the same, and I advise to experiment with both points of focus, and see which one works for you better. For some people, focus on the middle of the head is simpler than focus on their spine. For others focus on spine is more natural.

Make a note in your journal
How did the centering feel? Was it easy or difficult? Did you noticed any changes in your behavior after centering?

How To Ground

While centering is being used in order to make some psychic skill to work, next technique known as grounding is used mainly for protection – keeping your energy system safe at all time. The best way to describe it will be to refer to a lightning rod. When levels of psychic energies within your energy systems exceed the amount of energies your system can handle, you begun to suffer from a condition known as overload - this might result in tiredness, headaches, weakness and less control over psychic energies. In order to fix the problem, you have to get rid of the energies, so you turn yourself into such a lighting rod – you're releasing psychic energies into ground.

That's why this process is called grounding. When you sense that you sense you become overload, or you have other physical sensations you can't explain, it won't hurt if you try grounding. This technique is also important when you become a target for psychic attack of overload. So actually, how to ground yourself? There are three steps to do so.

1. **Center** - First you have to center yourself, and you already know how to do this.. Focus on perceiving the darkness within your closed eyes. Focus on this darkness, and think of the small point in the middle of your head. After few seconds, you should be well focused and centered. Therefore, you can move to the next step.
2. **Shift awareness to your feet** - When either standing or sitting, your feet should be touching the ground, either floor of the room, or grass in open space etc. You should already know what shifting awareness is, if you follow this book page by page. If you skipped few pages, please return and learn about New Energy Ways and Mobile Body Awareness. If you know what MBA is, then, as said earlier, use it to focus on your feet. Feel their shape, size and pressure of the body pushing them to the ground. Spend another few seconds to get the right feeling. Then move to the third and final step.
3. **Release the energy** - Again use Mobile Body Awareness to move the energy from your energy body down through your legs and through your feet into the ground. Continue moving the energy using tactile sensations into the ground for 5 to 15 minutes. Then just stop. Physical sensations should be gone, or they should start disappearing. If they don't, repeat grounding process. If the feelings won't go away even then, perhaps they're not caused by energy overload, or you found yourself under psychic attack and I would recommend leaving the area.

And this way you have learned how to ground yourself - another major step in energy work and psychics. You can also ground by hugging a tree. Trees are natural structures that collect spiritual, cosmic energies, and they transfer them to the ground. When you hug a tree, it also takes your energies back to the ground. When you have too much energy within your energy system, find a tree, and just hug it. It will not only take the energies you don't want, but it will also fill you with spiritual, cosmic energies, thus bringing your energies back to balance.

Make a note in your journal

Were grounding exercises difficult or not? How did you felt during grounding, and how did you felt after you've grounded your energies? Any differences or changes in your mood and emotional state? Any unusual sensations at all?

Energy Filtering

The last element of field maintenance is energy filtering. This skill is used to filter negative energies, which can be picked up from other people, or by spending even few minutes in a haunted house. Negative energies within your energy system can cause headaches or tiredness, aggression or depressive thoughts, or even illness of a different sort so it's important to get rid of these energies as soon as possible. The process isn't very different from grounding except one single step. In order to filter the energy, start normal grounding process, and when you're done with releasing the energy into ground, move to step number four.

1. Center
1. Shift awareness

2. Release the energy
3. **Draw fresh energy** - The negative energy is gone and there's enough space to draw new, fresh and positive energy. Therefore, use New Energy Ways to draw these new energies. You can use three ways to do so - through your hands, legs or through your central channel within spine. First two ways are already familiar to you, but the second one requires some explanation. Draw the energy, starting from the tip of your head, through your 7th chakra, then through your central spine channel, and into Lower Energy Center. Continue this process for few minutes. And that's is all.

Just remember to draw the energy in positive places, away from haunted locations and negative people. You might try to create a psychotronic device to for charging purposes, but it's more advanced subject. Practice with all these three skills for about a week now. Ground each day remembering not to push too far, so you won't get rid of all your energies. Center during meditation for a few minutes, or, when you're riding a bus or train, or waiting for someone or something. Finally, filter the energy few times a day. This will give you enough practical experience to move further.

Just Do It!

You don't really think if grounding, centering etc. really works – there's no point to do so, based on my observation and work with guinea pigs (my friends and students) I know it works even if you can't feel it. The very same thing will apply for further talents like psi-balls. You don't think "does it work?" - you trust yourself. There is a general rule – energy follow thoughts, so if you can think, you can also manipulate psychic energies.

The problem many face in case of psychic phenomena is that they can pick up information or manipulate psychic energies subconsciously – but they can't do the same consciously. Let me explain – when you can sense psychic energies, you know you have made psi-ball. But often, you can sense the psi-ball, but you're not aware of it. Subconsciously you say to yourself "OK, I can't sense anything, it doesn't work". That's where the trust comes in – you need to trust yourself, you need to trust you're doing things correctly. Then, your subconscious will give up, and you will begin to sense things.

The same thing applies to extra-sensory perception – you're picking up information during psychic reading, but you don't trust they're correct, so you're having problems understanding and interpreting them – and because of this, you think you don't experience any success in the field. Later, when you will read over Remote Viewing tutorials, you will learn a technique of picking up information, and you will also learn few techniques for picking up information during psychic readings and other clairvoyance skills, so don't worry about it now. Simple trust you can do this.

That's how things work – you learn energy manipulation, then you learn proper techniques for use of psychic ability, and at the same time, you're learning to trust your feelings – it's that simple. This is the path to become psychic.

Inward And Outward Energy Manipulation

When people begins to manipulate energy outside their body, they're facing a great problem - well, it's a small problem in reality, but huge one in their eyes. They just can't see anything. For some reasons, beginner energy workers expect to see the energy they're manipulating when they're pushing it outside their bodies. I do not know if it's because of TV or because of things they've read in the web, but the truth is, until you're a mutant of some sort, you won't see the psychic energy. With time you might develop the ability to see auras, but seeing psychic energies is an advanced psychic skill. Of course, there are rumors about the phenomena known as 'flaring', but I will discuss this later, in another part of this book. For now, just know that there's no way to see psychic energies, so don't worry if you won't see them when practising psychics - it's very normal, and there are no reasons to be concerned.

There's an interesting question regarding outside energy manipulation. With Mobile Body Awareness, you can feel your physical body, and this is understandable. But how to manipulate the energy outside your body using New Energy Ways? My answer is simple - the same way you manipulate it in your body.

Exercise: Sit down and face the wall, which should be located about half a meter in front of you. Close your eyes, and use Mobile Body Awareness to focus on your dominant hand. Now pick up your hand - but not the physical one, the energy hand - it feels like moving your physical hand, and you can move it just like you can move its physical counterpart. Now use the energy body hand to touch the wall - feel the texture of the wall. You will be surprised with the results. Try to touch your whole room this way. Just like you can manipulate your energy body inside, you can manipulate your energy body outside - the principles are the same.

Now, at last you can make another step in your psychic development – open your chakras – the primary energy centers.

Opening & Balancing Chakras

"Let's Roll"

Now you're getting to more advanced energy body development. You're going to develop chakras. It is extremely important that you follow this section of the book carefully, because chakras stimulation might be dangerous for your energetic and physical and mental health. Do not experiment, do not play around until you really know what you're doing. Really stick with the exercises on following pages carefully.

The Seven Chakras

As you already know from the previous chapters of this book about energy body, Chakras are energy centers within the energy system, and there are seven of them located along your spine. Below is a short review of these chakras, their colors and spiritual fields they're responsible for, based on Hindu beliefs. I know you have already learned the details about chakras, but as you know, repetition is the key to memorizing things, so here we go again.

- **Root Chakra** - The red chakra that grounds and connects us to the earth. This chakra focuses on basic needs like food, shelter, and water, and general physicality.
- **Abdomen Chakra** - The orange chakra that goes round in our lower abdomen, right below the navel. This chakra is associated with health, pleasure, feelings, and sexuality.
- **Solar Plexus Chakra** - The yellow chakra heats up our personal sense of power. Located at the solar plexus, this chakra helps to center us.
- **Heart Chakra** - The green chakra, which helps us feel love and compassion toward ourselves. It's the "love" chakra.
- **Throat Chakra** - The blue energy center spins its truth in our throat, helping us to be authentic in the way we live our lives.
- **Third Eye Chakra** - The violet light of this chakra makes its mark on our forehead, between the eyebrows and slightly above. This is where we see, where our inner eye lives.
- **Crown Chakra** – The bright white light glows at the top of our head, radiating upward, reaching its rays out

into the world beyond us. This is the most spiritual chakra of all.

The name "Chakra" originates comes from Sanskrit and means vortex (yes, you're right, previously I mentioned that the term originates from Hindu beliefs. But of course, Hindu beliefs have a lot in common with Sanskrit language). Chakras are responsible for maintaining physical balance of our body, energy balance of our energy system and spiritual balance of our mind and spirit. Normally, chakras are closed, or in other words, almost none developed. Stimulating them will force them to develop (open) and to utilize more energy, and utilize it more effectively. The more energy they can utilize and the more they're developed, the more information you can acquire via psychic means, possible developing such abilities are clairvoyance or clairaudience in an advanced form. While energy exchange ports in feet or palms are responsible for sensing and drawing energy, it is the responsibility for chakra to "translate" the energy into psychic impression.

Opened and balanced chakras lead not only to psychic development, but they can also improve your life in every single aspect of it. That's why psychic development has a lot in common with spiritual growth. Continue your work with the chakras, and soon you should notice many changes in your life. First, you will learn how to energize your chakra. This, as always, might lead for re-emerging of negative patterns. So, keep this in mind and be ready for new affirmations and further emotional healing work.

Chakra Stimulation

For the next few months, along with standard energy work learned in the chapter about New Energy Ways, you will add one more 15-minutes exercise to your practice schedule. It will deal only with stimulation of a single chakra. We will start small, from the root chakra, and then move chakra by chakra from the bottom to the top. During chakra stimulation, you might feel real physical sensations such as warm, tingling, pressure or even pain. It's very normal, and it should not worry you, because nothing bad will happen to your energy system nor physical body.

One more thing you need to remember. Chakras cannot be closed, at least not entirely. It's a common misconception that was born among new-agers who didn't really understood the rules of chakras opening (they would know if they would ever pay attention to learning). It's a simple thing. Any chakra can be open through energetic stimulation. And stimulation is based on thoughts, and tactile sensations, as well. But in order to close a chakra, you would have to think about it and feel it using tactile sensations, right? And when you do, guess what - you stimulate it. And that's it. You can't really close chakra intentionally, but the activity of specific chakra can be decreased, by following simple rules:

- **Calm down** - take few deep breaths and count down from 10 to 0, then release the tension.
- **Think about something else** - don't think about the chakra, think about something else like the work you have to do or a pleasant evening you had few days earlier.
- **Take a walk** - go for a walk, this will relax you and take thinking about chakra away.
- **Go jogging** - something similar to taking a walk, but a little faster.
- **Take a shower** - either hot or cold, whichever you prefer.

But you can control what kind of energies flow into your chakra, by placing intention filters on them. It's like creating artificial blockages, but this time you're not blocking any positive thoughts, you're just blocking negative thoughts. This can be achieved by re-programming you mind – something that you're doing from the very beginning of this book. The more positive thoughts you have, the less negative energies influence you. That's all. Now, we can move to actual exercises.

How To Open A Chakra

Now, to the actual stimulation process. We're going to start with the root chakra. Take a look at the image on the right to locate it. In order to stimulate it, we have to use New Energy Ways technique, to be more specific - some brushing and tearing actions. Below is a step by step guide.

- **Center -** The first step is to center. Centering has been discussed in an earlier part of this book so go back and read it again if you forget what it is. When centered, focus on that little dot inside your head and clear your mind, do not think about anything specific. After few seconds of focusing, let's move forward. There is no need for any particular trance, or deep meditation state is required for chakra stimulation, as NEW is always easy and simple to use.
- **Focus on the chakra** – Now think of the chakra you're about to stimulate. In this case, it's the root chakra, and you already know where it is. If you can't locate it with your mind, use the image and your finger and touch this part of your body, literally feel it with your physical senses. Do this first with eyes open, and then with eyes closed, pay attention to all feelings, but most important,

pay attention to location of the chakra you're stimulating.
- **Circles & Tearing** – Now using New Energy Ways, it means using tactile sensations, literally feel how you make a circles around that chakra. That is why it's important to learn how to operate NEW first, and then move here. If you haven't explored New Energy Ways yet, go few pages back and read that part. If you have practiced NEW, now touch the chakra location with your finger and make few circles around. Feel the touch, and the finger making circles on your skin. Then take your finger away, but keep feeling the circles. When you feel them just with your mind, then you're using NEW. After about 5 seconds of making circles, tear the chakra – feel the physical sensations of the energy center being opened wide – do this for another 5 seconds, then get back to making circles. Perform the whole process of stimulation for 10 to 15 minutes.

Stimulation of all other chakras looks the same. You just replace the chakra that you're stimulating. From personal experience, I can tell that probably the most difficult to stimulate is the second chakra. But all others are fairly easy, with root and brow chakras on the top of this easiness list. Let's get to the actual schedule, each chakra should be stimulated for one month, from 10 to 15 minutes per day. Again – work with chakras for 5 days, then take the weekend off. And remember the schedule isn't set in stone, if you believe you could use few more weeks of chakra work, do so.

Schedule

30 days per each chakra, 15 minutes
Total of 7 months, 1 month for each chakra

Month	Chakra	Additional Information
1	Root	One of the most important chakras to open, pay great attention to it. It might give you some intense physical sensations.
2	Abdomen	This one might be difficult to sense, but keep working on it for a month time.
3	Solar Plexus	It's a strong and powerful chakra, pay attention to its stimulation.
4	Heart	It might not be easy to sense it at first, but stimulate it anyway.
5	Throat	It might give you some weird sensations around your throat, but don't worry – everything is OK.
6	Third Eye	Probably most important chakra to stimulate, required for psychic work.
7	Crown	It's an enigma, hard to describe, but again work with it anyway.

After few months, you can either focus completely on practising psychic talents, or you can start stimulating your chakras all again, and see where it might lead you – it's not mandatory, as after seven months you can forget about chakras, and it won't make a big difference. Yet it's good to spend one week per each few months and stimulate all the chakras again. Especially after some serious illness, because they might get weaker due to the physical weakness.

Make a note in your journal

How did chakra stimulation feel? Keep a journal of chakra opening as well, pay attention to all sensations and unusual experiences. Note when there are better and worse days in your development. Can you notice similarities between good days, and similarities between bad days?

Other Ways Of Stimulating And Balancing Chakras

Of course, energy manipulation is not the only way to manipulate chakras. You can also use breathing techniques, mandalas, mantras and colors to stimulate and balance your chakras. I will discuss these methods now.

You can stimulate and balance your chakras through music, mantra, colors, crystals and scents. Just by listening to specific music; staring at specific color; or placing specific crystal on the chakra; all of this can help balance the energies in your chakras. Below, you can see a table for all the seven chakras, and different means of balancing them.

Chakra	Music	Mantra	Color	Crystal	Scent
Root	Music with slow,	Lam	Red	Ruby, Red Coral, Red Jasper, Agate	Clove, Cedar

	monotonous rhythms				
Sacral	Folk music	Vam	Orange	Moonstone, Carnelian	Sandal, Ylang-Ylang
Solar Plexux	Orchestral music, powerful rhythms,	Ram	Yellow, Gold	Topaz, Tiger Eye, Amber	Bergamot, Rosemary, Lavender,
Heart	Classic music, sacral music	Yam	Pink, Green	Jade, Emerald, Pink Quartz, Tourmaline,	Rose Oil
Throat	New Age Music, Vocals	Lam	Blue	Aquamarine, Chalcedony, Turquoise	Eucalyptus
Third Eye	Peaceful Ambient music, classic music	Aum	Transparent indigo, transparent blue	Lapis Lazuli, Sodalite	Mint, Jasmine
Crown	Silence	Om	Purple, White	Amethyst, White Quartz	Lotus

Mandalas & Mantras

You can also use mandalas and mantras for additional stimulation of your chakras. Mandalas are simple paintings that can be used to support your meditation. By focusing on the mandala, and on the chakra that this mandala represents, you stimulate your chakra. You can find mandalas for different chakras in esoteric stores on-line. You just place such painting in front of you, and you focus on in during your meditation.

Mantras, on the other hand, are sounds you 'vibrate'. It means that you need to pronounce them in this specific way, so your whole throat vibrates. The best way to learn this is to go on-line, and listen to the chants of Tibetan monks. Each chakra has one mantra assigned to it. When you sit down, and you vibrate the mantra for few seconds. During each 'run', you should vibrate each mantra 108 times. To keep a track, Buddhist practitioners used so called malas, a form of Buddhist rosary. Vibrations of teach mantra and focus on the chakra the specific mantra represents is another way of stimulating and balancing your chakra.

You can use these additional methods of stimulation and balancing along with the energy practice. Just a word of caution, do not practice anything that you have "designed" on your own, or anything that your inexperienced buddy shared with you. Chakra stimulation is a gentle work. Don't speed things up. Be gentle, stick to the schedule, and remember about affirmations and emotional healing.

Psychic Work

"Words are the fog one has to see through."

After few months of working with your chakras, affirmations and core images, you can start to learn practical psychic abilities. With time and practice, the below exercises will be easier to perform, but even now, they should give you no problems. What you're going to learn, is a set of psychic techniques that utilize your intentions, thoughts and energy manipulation to achieve specific things. For example, read someone's aura, or perform psychometry. Remember to use your intuition during the exercises. And if your intuition tells you to do things differently than I have written, then listen to your intuition. Maybe you can use your intentions and energy manipulation in a different way, so you can get better results.

How To Sense Energy

We will start with the ability to sense psychic energies consciously. Sometimes you will sense these energies even if you won't want to, this is called passive sensing. Intentionally sensing the energy is called active sensing. There are two areas of your body that works best for active sensing: palms of your hands and your spine. For now, we will deal with sensing using hands.

Shifting Awareness Technique

Which hand should you choose? Personally I'm using my none-dominant hand, for a simple reason - it sense energy better. How to tell which of your hands sense energy better, should become obvious while practising new energy ways. More developed hand will give you no problems with energy manipulation. The energy will flow with easy, and you will sense it better than in case of your less developed hand. But as I've noticed, for some people it's not such obvious so do not stick with the rule: none-dominant hand equals better energy sensing, because maybe in your case it is your dominant hand that is developed more than any other part of your body. The answer will come to you with practice, so don't worry if you can't really tell now which hand you should be using, experiment with both for now.

Now let's get to practice. Choose the hand, which you will use to sense the energy now. You don't really need the source of this energy for now, because we will deal with that later. For now, it will be something like cold practice. What we need now is to shift awareness. It's the same thing as practising NEW. You just focus on the specific part of your body entirely. Focus on your hand, and forget about everything else. Pay attention only to your hand. Feel its shape, size, position, every single move, focus totally on this part of your body. Keep your focus for few minutes for the first time. This is how shifting awareness looks like as you already know – I hope you haven't forgot anything about Mobile Body Awareness. Your awareness can be shifted to other parts of your body as well, like your ear, leg, single finger etc. Or it can be shifted to objects that aren't part of your body, too - but it's more advanced subject, and we will not deal with it in this book. But as you remember, you already tried moving the energy to touch the wall during one of previous exercises.

Now that your awareness shifted to your hand, begun energy work, stimulate your hand using new energy ways, both brushing and circling. Do this for few minutes. This is what is called "warming up", and with time, you will be able to warm up within seconds.

After warming up, keep your focus on your hand. Pay attention to all the feelings you have. Energy exchange ports in your hand are now stimulated, and they can easily sense psychic energy wherever you place your hand. Try this, move your hand from place to place. Try to sense how the emptiness of the room feels like, how your bed feels like, how the plant radiate with psychic energies etc. Try this exercise in both inside different buildings, on the street and in the wild - in a forest or while staying on a cornfield. Different places, different people and different times of a day will have different "feeling" - this is called the psychic energy signature. Now this is a complex subject of psychic Science and we will not get into details, for now just play around for few days and practice the technique of sensing few times a day.

Soon, you will feel a difference in your sensing abilities, and you will notice you awareness of psychic energies start to increase.

But those are hands – what about sensing the energy with central channel in the spine? While hands can be targeted to specific objects, it would be hard to target your spine, right? Exactly – that's why hands are mainly used for active sensing, while spine is a tool for passive sensing – sensing the energy with spine is simple, and it limits itself to shifting awareness and warming up the central energy channel – et voila.

Anyway, for basic energy work stick with sensing energies with your hands, as it will be very useful talent in just few moments – you're going to learn how to create the famous psiball.

There's just one more thing, that I need to mention. Energy sensitivity, it is an ability to sense psychic energies in general, and not just with your hands. Don't worry about this, though. With time, your sensitivity will develop further. Again, do not expect to sense energies in any specific way. Some people "smell" energies, some "see" them, and some just know there the energies are there. With time, you will learn.

Creating A Psiball

With knowledge about energy sensing, it's time to learn how to manipulate psychic energy outside your body. In order to do so, you will now learn how to create a psiball.

What Is A Psiball

Psiball is the most basic energy construct that can be created by manipulating psychic energy. As stated by the name itself, it's a ball of psychic energy formed between hands. It can be created no matter what's your development level, because as basic construct, it's just a ball, but as advanced construct, it can be programmed to do multiple things. Making psiball is the first really practical thing you're going to make using energy manipulation, so pay attention and have fun, because no matter what, psiball is so old school.

Psiballs don't have many uses, really. But the creation of a psiball is a great training exercise that can teach you a bit about energy manipulation. The knowledge you will gain now, will be very useful later on, for example, in psychic readings, or psychic healing.

What is a construct? It's a thing made of psychic energy, or to put it in simpler words – a shape of psychic energy, like a ball, cube, a brick, or even a flower. The shape of construct depends only on the skills of your imagination. Literally everything can be created using energy manipulation techniques. And every single construct can be programmed.

Programming Of Energy Constructs

Just like operating system tells a computer what to do, and DNA code tells living beings how to grow, program of energy construct tells the construct what to do. For example, I can program the psiball to fly around the room, hang in the west corner and remain there until its energy is depleted. Or I can tell it to hang there and draw energy from the nearest pyramid charger and by this, remain there forever (pyramid charger is a psychotronic device, will be described with more details near the end of this book).

How the programming is done? It's all about the intention, your thoughts you keep in your mind when creating a construct. Putting these intentions into a construct is called programming. Programming is very simple, when creating a construct, meaning moving the energy and manipulating it into a specific shape, at the same time keep the intention inside your mind, think what you want the construct you're making to do. And that's all you really need to know - keep the intention, literally know what the thing you're creating will do in few seconds. After all, programming is all about intend, and your Will to do something. It's that simple.

Programming is a complex process. Few pages from here I will give some additional tips regarding this subject, though. For now, let's get back to our psiball.

Creation Process

Making a psiball isn't difficult, now that you know how to draw and manipulate energy in your body, you're going to do the very same things, but this time, outside your body. You are going to use New Energy Ways system to move the energy from your lower energy storage center, move it through your arms to a space between your palms. Let's begin!

Sit down and clear your mind. Close your eyes and center. Then move your point of focus to the lower storage center and feel this tan t'ien. Use New Energy Ways method to move the energy (using tactile sensations) up to your both arms at the same time, then down to your both hands, and then finally feel the energy moving outside your body to a space between your palms. When you feel the energy moving outside, it's time to program it.

Keep the intention of the energy forming a shape of a ball, a ball that hangs between your palms at all time. Keep this intention while still moving new waves of energy from your tan t'tien through arms and hands into the space between palms. Those are two most important things - intention of creating a ball, and adding new energy you collected through your NEW practice. Keep forming the ball and adding energy for about 3 to 5 minutes.

After this time, finally stop moving the energy, and stop thinking about forming a ball. It's time to sense the psiball you have just created. Focus on the space between your hands. Try to move them toward each other – do you feel any pressure? Or any other sensations like cool, warm, tingling, or anything else? If you do feel something, then you have created your very first psiball. If you don't feel anything, then you will just have to try again. The sad true is that creating a psiball for the first time isn't the easiest thing in the world, even if you have strong energy manipulation skills. Just like you have learned to sense and manipulate energy in your body, you have to spend some time practising to learn how to sense the energy outside your body.

No matter if you were successful in creating a psiball or not, it's time to practice new talent on a daily basis. Continue to create at least one psiball per day for another month. It's all about getting better and better in energy manipulation. If you want, you can try making up to 10 psiballs per day, but beware, it might be dangerous for your energy system. If you feel tired, stop making psiballs. There always is another day. There's a saying: one psiball, two psiballs, three psiballs, four... five psiballs, six psiballs, seven psiballs, floor.

You can also practice making psiballs using simple Qi Gong exercise. It's even simpler than classic method of psiball creation described earlier. Stand up, bend your knees a little and extend your hands in front of you, with your palms facing each other. Leave about 15 inches of space between your hands and start breathing - when you breath in, move your hands away. When breath out, feel and intend to gather the energy between your hands and press it into a shape of a ball. Continue to gather and press the energy for about 5 minutes. This is a nice exercise because it can be performed everywhere and nobody will laugh at you, as you can explain you're practicing breath exercises.

Make a note in your journal
How did the psi-ball feel? What kind of sensations did you experience? How long did it take before you successfully created the psi-ball?

After a month of practice, you will feel the psiball between your palms for sure, and you will be able to move further.

Flaring – Making Things Visible

One day I've been asked a question: "what is flaring?" - the answer is very simple. Flaring is making the energy construct visible to the naked eye. It's complicated, because there's not enough proofs to tell if the phenomena really takes place, but even if it does, two more questions must be answered: does the flare is visible to every person capable of seeing, or can it be perceived only by people who can perceive aura (the skill is called aura view - the ability to see aura of living beings and material objects).

There is no real answer to question 'how to flare'. Some people say that if you draw enough energy to the construct, it will flare. But since most people who say this also admit that 'some people just do not have the gift of flaring', I wouldn't recommend learning anything more about the skill of flaring or the phenomena itself as long as you're just a beginner in energy work.

I can remember my first flaring. I was sitting in my room with only weak light, so it was pretty dark. I spent about 6 minutes on making the psiball with my eyes closed. When I opened them, it's pretty normal they were tired. But when I took a look at my hands, a space between them to be more specific, I saw a shape of a ball, "build" of thousands of particles flying around between both my hands. They were week, but I clearly see the shape of a ball - it wasn't shining, to be honest, it was nearly invisible, but I count it as my first (and only) flaring.

I do this because I connect the facts. Aura, which is nothing more nor less than our energy field which is build of the same energy as psiball, is more visible when the eyes are tired - being tired forces the "third eye" to perceive the energy in psychic way because physical eyes are unable to do this. It's yet-another way to trick your brain.

But, because I was not able to repeat the process and I have never flared again, I do not consider this skill to be important in any way - it's interesting, but not very practical. If you want, you can pursuit further.

So, as I said - flaring, if real, isn't very practical, especially if you still are a beginner. When you get better after many months, perhaps years of practice, you can get back to the subject. Until then, stick with energy manipulation without trying to see the energy.

More On Programming

Because we're now going to get into details of energy constructs, you have to learn a bit more about constructs programming. Programming makes psychics not very different from magic - programming is a psychic term used for passing out intend into the energy - something that happens in magic using rites, spells and accessories like wands. The best way to explain what programming is will be to bring the example of a computer program - while the computer is a machine, and electricity is the fuel it operates on, the program is a way to tell the machine how to move electricity around to perform specific tasks. And the program is being created by our own mind.

So here we come to the term of intention - let's take the psiball, for example, what do you want it to do? Move across the room and stop? Then think about psiball moving across the room and stopping - and that's programming, because it was your desire, your intend for the psiball to perform this specific task. And this intend can be small or big - you can intend the energy construct to move across the room, or fly to the town center, hang somewhere in the mall and collect information about every single person visiting this mall - it's theoretically possible, because that's what intend is. In case of practical possibility, then it would require a lot of practice.

How to program the construct? Actually you already know this - you have created a psiball. When you were moving the energy into the area between your palms, it was your intend that the energy forms into a shape of a ball - so you programmed the energy to become the ball. And that's pretty it - intend that is kept in mind while manipulating the energy is the energy programming.

Visualization

Additionally, you can add visualization support to programming - which means you can literally visualize in front of your eyes the whole program. What is visualization? Close your eyes and try to see, for example, an orange (the fruit of course, not the color) – do it right now. Can you see it? Good, you have visualized an orange. Basically, visualization is a process of imagining something in front of your eyes – an object, a person, an event – anything.

Next thing you should know is that there many different levels of visualization – you can "just" see your orange, but you can also smell it, touch it or taste it. Everything depends on how strong you can visualize (as you can... see, visualization sometimes have nothing to do with visual data). There is an interesting aspect of this process. Your mind doesn't recognize if you are just visualizing an orange, or that you have it in front of you on your table, for real. There were many experiments, in which sports mans were visualizing themselves during a race, and their organisms were acting as they were racing for real. So when you're visualizing something, your mind think it's real.

It's all the same when it comes to psychics – if you're visualizing a psiball, for example, your mind is thinking this energy ball is real. Of course, you might say "maybe I'm lying to myself?". Maybe – but then how could you explain psiballs affecting electronic equipment, moving thinks using psychokinesis or reading other's minds? Because all of this is real; when your mind is thinking it's real, it will be – for real…

Exercise: Keep your eyes open. Now, DO NOT think about your kitchen, do not think about your fridge in your kitchen, do not think about all this stuff in your fridge, do not… whoh, wait a minute – you saw your kitchen? And you saw your fridge? As you can see, you can not "not use" this ability, it's a natural part of your mind – you are visualizing everything all over the time. Yet you can improve this ability simple by practising – visualize your kitchen again, try to smell dinner, try to hear voices, try to open the fridge etc.

Visualize everything and everywhere – you will get better and better with practice. The visualization is an important skill in case of psychic programming. We will use it now to create and program a defensive psychic shield.

Psychic Self-Defense

I would say that when you start manipulating the energy, you become a target for astral entities of a different sort, but I won't say that. OK, in reality you won't become a target right away, and more probably you won't become a target at all. It's just that sometimes you might encounter psychic vampires on your way (people who can drain you out of psychic energy), or you might found yourself in a haunted location where entities like spirits or astral critters might consider you as a battery, and they will use you to charge themselves. Or finally, you might become a target for other psychic practitioner or a witch or an occult practitioner because you weren't nice enough, and they might try to attack you using psychic means. That's why it's an important step to take to learn psychic defenses. Psychic Self-Defense is about defending yourself against psychic phenomena.

It's not like psychics aren't good people. But there are many types of energy workers out there, who get their abilities not through spiritual growth, but by practicing dark arts such as black magick. And there are also different astral entities that wonder around on the astral planes. So it's good idea to learn few things about psychic self-defense.

The basic way to create a psychic shield is to visualize yourself being surrounded by pure, white light, and intend this light to be your spiritual protection. Through this simple technique, you can create the basic psychic shield, your basic way of psychic self-defense. But there are more advanced ways to create psychic shields, as well.

Psychic Shielding

Psychic shields are the basic method of psychic self-defense. Basically, they're like psiballs - they're constructs made of psychic energy formed around your body, meant to protect you.

There are two primary types of psychic shield. First is called a "bubble" shield and it is a construct in shape of a bubble around your physical body and most of your energy field. The second type of psychic shield is a skin layer shield, and this type is an energy shield formed few inches above the skin, and it doesn't cover your energy field entirely.

Either bubble or skin layer shield can be programmed in different ways. The number of programs vary from person to a person as it is limited to ones imagination, but there are two primary types of programming.

- **Absorb Shield** – This type of shield is meant to absorb all the energies that hit it. Therefore, the more energy hits it, the stronger the shield becomes, because it absorbs and utilize the energy to power itself. The problem with this shield program is that it might overload because of the amount of energy that has been absorbed, and when it does overload, it might damage the energy system of your own body. There's also second type of programming.
- **Mirror Shield** – This shield is meant to reflect all the energy that hit it. It's not free of "malfunctions" as we also have a small problem with it. Because the energy being reflected cannot be targeted, as it's not ours and we have no control over it, so it might hit everything and everyone around you - from the enemies to friends. Yet in my opinion, it probably is the best defense shield that is possible to being created.

How To Make A Psychic Shield

Below you can find another practical technique for learning new psychic ability - psychic shielding. Follow the technique step by step, and you shall have your shield ready in a matter of minutes.

- **Defining the goal** – Depending on the situation you're facing, you might want to create either an absorb or a mirror shield. Define which one you want to create. For example, if you're under psychic attack, which is strong, and your own energy manipulation and programming skills aren't the best, perhaps mirror shield will be better than absorb shield as the absorb shield is harder to program. If the attack is weak or you feel OK with your energy manipulation skills, then probably absorb shield is the one for you to choose.

- **Centering** – As with almost every single psychic technique first step to take is to center your mind and focus. Do this before moving to the next step.
- **Drawing energy** – Use your favorite energy manipulation system to draw the psychic energy into your LTT. For New Energy Ways practitioners who follow this book, remember to draw the energy into your first energy storage (LTT) below the stomach. If you believe you already have enough energy to create a shield, simple skip that step and move further.
- **Setting the intention** – Now decide what you want - it's time to prepare the program for the shield. Keep this intend either to create a shield that will absorb all or only specific types of energies, so it will become stronger, or to create a shield that will reflect all the energies (or only specific types of energies, for example, negative or energies carrying emotions). You already know what programming is, so this step should be easy.
- **Rising the shield** – Now, feel the energy (using your favorite energy manipulation system) rising up through your main energy channel in the spine to the tip of your head, then outside for about 15 centimeters above your head, then down like a water from the fountain falling to the ground, entering it and finally turning and

moving back through your legs and lower parts of the primary channel back to the LTT. At the same time, feel or visualize the energy spinning around you, while keeping the intend for the shield inside your mind at all time. Continue the process of rising the shield from few seconds to few minutes.
- **Shelling** - When the shield is finally up, it's time to shell it – feel or visualize the shield becoming hard, impenetrable (this process is called shelling which you already know) and after you're done with visualization, you're done with setting the shield.

After months of practice of shielding, the entire process will take you less than few seconds.

Lowering The Shield

When the shield isn't needed because the attack is over or you're no longer in any haunted location, it should be "lowered", which means it should be destroyed. The process of lowering the shield is very simple:

- **Have an intend to lower the shield.**

Feel or visualize the shield disappearing, while keeping the intend of lowering it in your mind. Let the energy creating the shield become weaker and move entirely into the LTT. It's already rising up from the LTT, so just break the energy flow and let all of the energy return into the LTT.

As you can see, both setting up, and lowering the psychic shield is very easy and in most cases. It's possible to achieve a success for the first time you try the above. Remember, it's all about the intend and energy manipulation, and we all know that energy follow thoughts.

Psychic shields can be also created around other people and objects, from simple expanding the shield over, or expanding and leaving it there, like a soap bubble. To do so, visualize or use the Mobile Body Awareness to move the energy to cover something with it.

How will you know you have successfully created a shield? Well, until you become very sensitive to psychic energies, you won't know for sure until someone with proper psychic skills scans you. When you develop sensitivity, you will be able to sense the shield around you. Before this, you might feel like being in a closed space.

I recall an interesting experience that I was able to add to my "personal proofs" list. A psychic – Drea - has been giving me a reading, yet was unable to acquire much information because she faced my psychic shield set up - it appeared to her as gate that was closed, and when she tried to walk through it, a strong impression of "stay away!" has hit her. What she faced was my regular shielding that I use each day. As you can see, psychic shielding can be used also to block psychics from reading you.

Make a note in your journal

Have you felt anything unusual after successfully creating psychic shield? Did you felt like in tide room, or was there no difference at all? If you felt the shield, how many hours had passed before it depleted itself?

Wards

While psychic shield is an active method of psychic self-defense, sometimes we need to defend a place against both other people and even astral entities when we're not really there. In such case, we can use energy construct we call a Ward. Wards are energy constructs meant to perform specific tasks and just like psiball they can be programmed to do this. Think of them as of sentry turrets in computer strategy game. Such sentry turret is programmed to attack everything in a range that isn't an ally. You can program a Ward to do the same - sometimes it's attack, sometimes it's just repelling and scaring things away, like a warning sign. A Ward can be a place in a room, corridor, garden, somewhere in the forest etc. And it will remain there, as long as it is provided with an energy source to fuel itself.

In order to create a ward, you need to learn how to create and program a psiball first, which you have already done with, all you have to do is to program it properly.

How To Create Ward

Two things are required to create a Ward - programming and psiball. Fortunately, you already know both elements so follow this technique step by step, and you should create a Ward in a matter of minutes.

- **Define the goal** – First you have to decide why do you want to create the Ward. Do you want to scare bugs away? Or reflect all the negative energies hitting your room? Or repel negative entities out of the location? This is the first step, to define the goal and keep the intention within your mind. This is the beginning of Ward programming. Define the and keep it in your mind.
- **Create a psiball** – Now create a simple psiball in your hands using the technique described previously in this book, by moving the energy from Lower Tan T'ien through your hands to space between your palms to create a shape of a ball. While creating this psiball, still

keep in mind your intention you defined in step 1. You're now programming the Ward. On this step, you must add additional intention to your Ward - you have to decide where you will place your Ward and how it will behavior itself. For example, you can think of placing the Ward in the west corner of your room while putting more and more energy into the psiball - this way you will program where the ward should place itself. As for behavior - you need to answer two questions - will the Ward be stick to a specific place, or will it move around? And how will it regain psychic energy for fueling itself? At this stage of your training don't worry about moving Wards, stick with static ones, and as for the source of power, let the Ward burn all the energy it's made of and be gone - we will deal with an energy source at the end of this book.

- **Send the Ward away** – Now that the psiball is created and programmed, you have to send it on its way, in other words, you have to place it the place you've programmed. Just keep the intention to release the psiball and place it where it should be placed and push it there using both your intention and physical body - I mean, use your hands to push the ball. That completes the creation process, and your Ward should start working.

And that's it – the Ward is done. There's one more thing you will learn now. It can be used to improve not only your Wards, but also psychic shields, psiballs and other energy constructs. It's called shelling.

Shelling

Shelling is about putting a construct inside of another construct - and that's the best way to describe it. The difference between these two constructs is simple. Primary construct such as Ward is programmed to do something like, for example, repel spiders. Other construct known as Shell is meant to hold the energies of the first construct together, so they won't burn out too fast. Creating Shell is simple. Let's take the Ward as an example - after step 2 when you're about to release the Ward, hold on for a minute. Draw more energy creating second level of the Ward - the Shell. Now program it, keep the intend that the Shell will hold the energies inside of it and won't allow them to be drained out. After few seconds, add one more intend, this time your intend should be for Shell to crystallize, turning into a shield hard as diamond that can't be breached by other than primary Ward energies.

And this way you've created a Shell. Such shells can be added as support for Wards, psiballs, shields and other energy constructs, as well. Experiment with a new technique for few days and get used to it.

What Can You Use Wards For

Wards can be used for many things and here's a small list of examples.

- **Repel Spiders** - if you're afraid of spiders, put few Wards that will repel them. I've tested it on myself, and it works.
- **Repel Astral Critters** - Astral Critters are creatures from lower astral planes. Use the Ward to repel them to keep your place clean and out of negative energies.

- **Attack** - you might try Wards to defend your property. When a thief is about to enter your house, the Ward could release all its energy into his energy system, overloading it.
- **Attract** - or let's try a different approach, try to program Ward to attract girls, for example.

Can you see where I'm getting at with this? Wards can have multiple uses, and the only thing that limits you is your own imagination.

Psychic Attacks

Now you know how to defend yourself, but what kind of danger you might face when you are energy worker? This section is not meant to teach you how to attack someone with psychic skills, but rather educate you on types of dangers you might face and ways to defend against them.

The world isn't perfect, and there's a lot of dangerous things awaiting energy workers and psychics. Dangers like other people or natural high concentration of energies, or even haunted places as finding yourself in such haunted area isn't a rare thing.

Drain

One of the most common dangerous situation is called a drain. This is a type of psychic attack, related to psychic vampirism in most cases, yet it can also be used by anyone who knows a thing or two about energy work. Drain is more or less simple. This is how it works: a person or entity drain the psychic energy directly from your energy system weakening it, and by doing so, the attack weakens your physical body, too As you recall, energy body is directly connected to the nervous system. The longer this attack last, the weaker you become. Continuous attack that last for weeks and months is capable of causing severe physical damages and illness such as anemia, for example.

As said, this attack might be carry out by psychic vampires, other energy workers, or entities in haunted places, but a place does not need to be "haunted", as entities can be found nearly everywhere.

How to defend yourself against this type of attack? Simple - set up a mirror shield, because in order to drain energy out of your system, the attacker must establish a link first (the nearly same type of energy link as you learned from this book). Still, one of the best-known ways to defend against drain attack is leaving the area where you're being attacked, as in most cases your attacker won't follow you - entities like an easy pray and a lot of psychic vampires isn't aware of their vampiric nature. You can also try to create a shield that will keep all your energy inside it – this way you won't easily allow it to be sucked out. Unfortunately, many entities and even people create links, so that the distance doesn't matter any more. In such case, you need to break the link. If you're advanced energy worker, you will be able to sense the link, and break it with your intention and energy manipulation. If you're not that experienced, then you need to find someone who can break the link for you.

Know this – in order to create links, one must find a way to attach himself (or itself). This is much harder to do in case of spiritual workers, who have worked with many of theirs emotional problems. There's not enough attachment points to create a link. Therefore, a great way of defending against this kind of attack is a continuous work with your core images.

Overload

While drain attack is like sucking energy out of you, overload attack is meant to pump additional energy into your system causing it to overload. As you should already know, energy system is directly connected to the nervous system. By overloading energy system, your physical, nervous system can be attacked as well, causing real physical damages of your body including physical pain - that's one this is one of the most dangerous psychic attacks. But those are only the strongest types of overload, as most of such attacks will just overload the system for few hours, by putting a way too much energy than the system can handle. Imagine that you are a closed bottle into which more and more water is being pumped. If the pressure reach a critical level, the bottle will explode. Of course, you will not explode, but too much energy flowing in your energy channels might cause headaches, diseases or troubles with energy manipulation.

How to defend against overload attack? Once again you should set up a shield that will be programmed to either reflect or absorb all the psychic energies that are being moved towards you. Additionally, you should ground yourself – as you remember, grounding has been discussed earlier this book. Grounding will move the exceeding amount of energies into the ground or just outside your energy system, which will make overload nearly impossible because all the energy entering your system will be removed from it within few seconds.

There are different sources of such overload psychic attack, here they are:

- **Other energy workers** – Whether they're psychics, mages or witches. Not every practitioner of the occult and new age arts have peaceful intentions. Everyone can learn how to manipulate psychic energies.
- **Astral entities** – Entities like spirits, astral critters or even demons can also launch such attack.
- **Location itself** – High concentration of psychic energies can be found in different areas of the world.

When unshielded, you might suffer from a form of "passive" overload when you simple find yourself in energy stream.

Haunted Places

Have you ever been in a haunted place such as cursed forest, house or flat, palace or castle? I performed many paranormal investigations, and I have visited many haunted locations, that's why I include the subject of haunting as a potential danger for energy workers.

Different entities might be operating in haunted place, from earthbound spirits that are trapped there, to astral critters that had entered out world through portals opened due to Ouija work, to demons - creatures of great power. All of these entities are dangerous for energy workers because they can initiate all kinds of previously mentioned psychic attacks.

They can also cause hallucination or embed fear inside your mind They can implant obsessive thoughts, or possess you. In order to defend against these types of psychic attacks, you should practice meditation in order to learn how to keep your mind disciplined. The subject of defending against astral entities is very complex, and there's simple no space here to discuss. I would have to write another book on the subject. For now, I recommend reading Practical Psychic Self-Defence by Robert Bruce, where he pointed many different methods of defending yourself against astral beings.

Sometimes entities from haunted places can follow you back to your own home. Therefore, do not play around haunted places if you're unprepared for the consequences. I don't say you shouldn't use your psychic skills to investigate the paranormal, but before doing so, learn what you might be dealing with and how you can defend against things you might encounter. From my own perspective, I recommend setting some Wards around your home that will keep entities of different away. You should already know it's not a big problem to create such Ward, a little bit of energy work and programming, and you're done.

Dangers In The Field

As I have mentioned, sometimes you might encounter high concentration of psychic energies, for example, around buildings, areas of space like rivers, forests, or group of stones. There are different, so-called places of power – some people refer this name to chakras of our planet (as there's a belief that our planet, too, have its own energy system just as we do). Others belief these places have been charged with psychic energies by some for of magic. Or there might be a high concentration of minerals underground, which causes psychic energies to focus in that specific area of space. No matter which explanation is real, the fact remains the same – by staying for a longer time in such area, you might expose yourself to either drain or overload. The best mean of defense in this case is to leave the area, therefore, if you sense there's something wrong with the energy around you, start making bigger steps.

A form of psychic attack is also: crop circles and shape-radiation objects. While most people believe that crop circles are made by aliens, this isn't true. The truth is that, beside crop circle makers, the real circles are more or less like acupuncture for planet Earth, a way of healing the energetic system and the environment. Crop circles that are real can be told from fake circles by the energetic imprint. To put it in simple words – when you will stand in the middle of a real crop circle, you will know it – as long as you're psychic sensitive. Circles like this are based on energetic sacred geometry and shape radiation (in a way). Basically, some shapes based on the rules of sacred geometry projects specific kind of energy that can be either positive or negative. Sometimes, this energy is quite spiritual;

thus, it can lead to removing subconscious blockages. But if the person isn't ready for changes, then the energy can be dangerous – it can lead to physical and mental illnesses. That's why even spiritual energies can be dangerous. If you're not ready for it, try to avoid crop circles, and energetic paintings, like spirals, for example.

Summary

Now you know what kinds of dangers you might encounter, and how to defend against them. We can move further and learn a bit about Extra-Sensory Perception.

Extra Sensory Perception

"If you light a lamp for someone, it will also brighten your own path."

Extra-Sensory perception is the ability to perceive information of a different sort, with no use of classic five senses like seeing or hearing. This is the thing often named as the sixth sense. When it comes to psychics, ESP is considered as wide category of different abilities that aren't meant to influence the physical reality, rather acquire information through different means. We recognize following abilities:

- **Clairvoyance** - an ability to perceive information visually.

- **Clairaudience** - an ability to perceive audio information.
- **Clairseintence** - an ability to sense psychic energies around you.

There are also skills than merge the above.

- **Psychometry** - a skill that helps acquiring information about physical objects and places via psychic means.
- **Telepathy** - a skill to communicate between two or more people or animals.
- **Remote Viewing** - a complex process of acquiring information about person, location and events.

But these are just the terms. Personally, I use the general term 'ESP', and I advise you to stick with this term, as well. Because in reality, clairvoyance and clairaudience often merge; telepathy isn't different from just knowing things; remote viewing is mixing psychometry, clairvoyance and telepathy together, as well. Generally, different terms only make things complicated, while the term 'ESP' points to the actual ability: to be psychically able to acquire information through psychic senses, and not through physical means.

And these 'psychic means' are simple: it's just using your intuition and intention together, in order to perform a specific task, like acquire information about a person or object. But, first things first, let's start with basic stuff.

Being Psychic Is About Awareness

When you start to develop your energy system, an ability of clairseintence will be the first to develop. You will become more sensitive to psychic energies around you, and this will be the first really important step in your psychic development. Can you recall any TV show about paranormal investigations that included a psychic on site? He or she must have said something like "I sense presence here" - and that's exactly what clairseintence is, sensing things. These things don't have to be conscious, so beside entities you can just sense streams or centers of psychic energies, but you can sense spirits and living people, as well.

Information is already there

All you have to do is to grab it! Sensing the energy around you is the first step - you already learn how to sense psychic energies in one of previous chapters of this book. Being able to use the sensing abilities is another issue. In a way, it's a perfect proof for development of your psychic abilities, first you haven't been able to sense much, after few months of energy work you can sense spirits, people, and flowing energies. The reasonable next step to make will be to learn how to acquire information from the energies you can pick up using your psychic senses. Within this part of the book, I will discuss few elements that are important for performing a real psychic reading, and few pages from here, I will explain with details how to perform such reading.

Different Forms Of Psychic Perception

Before we will move further to discuss psychic readings, psychometry and skills like that, you need to understand that there are different forms of psychic perception. In reality, psychics rarely hear or see things psychically with their physical senses. It is a common misconception that often leads to problems with learning any extra-sensory perception ability. People just don't understand that psychic sight is not the same as physical sight. If you want to be psychic, you need to understand that difference.

We need to redefine the word "see". Let me explain - there are many psychics out there that use the term "see" inappropriately. For example, a psychic medium during a seance might say "I see an older man standing next to you; it's your uncle Tom, who connected with our Lord three years ago". Now, do not be mislead by the word "see" - that psychic medium does not see anything, at least not with physical eyes. Another example - during psychic classes, some psychics ask they student to "feel the vibrations" - and students fail because they sense no vibrations. Now again, no psychic sense any vibrations, until a plane fly a bit too close to the ground.

However, there are psychics who can literally see spirits and energies with their physical eyes. How are they able to do so? To be honest, I have no idea. There are psychics who can literally feel physical sensations, and hear real sounds and voices. Personally, I do not see energies and energy bodies when I do psychic readings. I have a potential to do so, as I used to say, because when I was a teenager, I saw the spirit of my dad during his funeral, which I have mentioned it in the introduction to this book. He looked very real, exactly the same like at the time he died. Same hairs, same clothes, and if I wouldn't know he's dead, I wouldn't be able to distinct him from any other living person. But - I am not using my physical eyes to see energies. I'm using my inner psychic sight that is very similar to the ability of visualization, which everyone has.

During many past years, the way psychics discussed their psychic perception in books, or in TV, has led to many misinterpretation and problems. Psychic-wannabes do not understand what they should be expecting, and they are quite sad when they don't achieve the results they expect - some people might expect to see a ghost for real. Now OK, this is possible.

But if you don't want to fail in your psychic development process, you need to understand what you should be really expecting - so first all all, remember: you might not really see, hear, smell, feel or anything like that - this is reserved to your normal five senses in most cases. You might be lucky and awake such ability to use your physical senses to receive psychic input, but do not expect it. To be honest, do not expect anything at all - because you might program yourself to expect one thing, and you will never notice another form of psychic perception that you have awakened.

If you won't going to see or hear as you normally do, then how does psychic perception looks like in most cases? As I said, it's based on inner psychic senses.

You know there are these fancy terms like clairvoyance, clairaudience etc. In any case, that "clair" is what really matters. Think about it like a word that define your perception to be "inner perception". When I see things psychically, I either close my eyes, or keep them open. In any case, I see images, symbols, scenes like I would be visualizing things. You have learned about visualization earlier, so you understand what I'm talking about. Things I see aren't really clear. They could be, if you would be able to devote most parts of your brain into visualization process. But when you're awake, your brain have better, and more important things to do than improving your visualization. But you're capable of seeing things when you visualize consciously.

Psychic sight is the same - you see things as they would be visualized. But this time, you're not visualizing them consciously, you're letting your subconscious mind take control over the things you can perceive.

The same thing applies to psychic hearing. You don't hear real voices and sounds, but you hear things just like you hear your own thoughts. Say something in your mind - can you hear your "voice"? Well, this is psychic hearing. Sometimes it can be clear, sometimes it might be difficult to understand, but it is there.

Now it's hard for me to describe psychic physical sensations - because I haven't experienced them as I used to experience psychic sight or psychic hearing. When I sense something physically, I truly sense it physically. So I don't know what psychic physicality "feels" like, but I know that when I sense energies, I do sense temperature changes, tingling sensations and finally I often sense pressure.

Often, I also have that inner "feeling" that something isn't right. For no apparent reasons, I might get nervous or anxious or happy and relaxed. This is a way my body and psychic self to tell me what kind of energy flows around me. When I get negative feeling inside me, I recognize negative energies. And vice versa, when I get positive feelings inside me, I recognize positive energies. This ability can be often used to sense people. When you're around a person, and you feel good around that person, it means that either the room is filled with positive energies, or that the person projects positive energies. I don't have to explain how can you use this ability to sense if people project negative energies, right?

This is how psychic perception looks like. All types of extra-sensory perception, say - psychometry, clairvoyance, psychic readings, remote viewing and such, are only modifications of psychic perception - those are different techniques for acquiring information.

I need to mention one more thing. Often, many guides or teachers will tell you that you need to define your primary sense. Some people are visual; some prefer auditory input; some prefer touch and so on. Many books and teachers provide their students with exercises and tests that are meant to figure out which sense is dominant, so the person can use this knowledge to focus on perceiving psychic information through only one mean - for example, if someone is visual, he might want to choose to develop psychic sight only. Well, that might be true in case of some people, but sometimes you might be multi-sensual. And sometimes your primary psychic sense might be completely different from your dominant physical sense.

Therefore, do not fall into that trap of developing only one form of psychic perception. Be neutral, and stand in the middle. Work with psychic physical sense, psychic sight, psychic hearing, psychic smelling and any other psychic sense, because you never know which of your psychic senses can truly kick in, and become your dominant. Or, you might be surprised to discover that all your psychic senses are very strong and that they improve your overall psychic perception. Work with all your senses, instead of focusing on single one.

Introduction Technique

Before performing any form of ESP work, whether it's psychometry or psychic reading, or even any form of energy work, you should prepare yourself. To do so, you can use the following technique. Close your eyes, then ground and center yourself. Then, start breathing. Breathe slowly and gently, and relax all your muscles. Let go of all your thoughts. Count down from 10 to 0, and say to yourself, say in your mind, "*I'm now calm and relaxed. I am ready to perform my psychic work.*" This is an element of auto-programming of your mind. Perform this relaxation before each psychic work, to make sure your mind is ready.

Aura View

Every person got aura - it is a field of psychic energies that expand outside normal energy body - created by particles being projected from our own energy system. Because of this, because these energies have been cycled through our body, and our organs, it is possible to read the aura, and notice any emotional states or problems with physical or emotional bodies of a person. This is what many psychics call "aura reading".

Many psychics also say that aura got colors, and different colors represent a different type of feelings or physical states. They also say everyone can learn how to perceive colors of the aura. Well, here we face a huge problem - not everyone is able to see aura, and not everyone is capable of perceiving its colors. People who say everyone can see colors of auras are simple mislead, or don't understand this skill at all. And not everyone can see aura through physical eyes. Often, people can perceive aura and energy bodies (and energies in general) through their inner psychic sight only.

Multiple Aura View Layers

There are multiple layers of so called "aura view". Most people can't see aura, nor they can see any psychic energies with their physical eyes - that's why I didn't want to teach this skill anywhere in this book, at first. Some people can see auras as mist, or waving air (like hot air hovering about hot surface). Some people can perceive aura as millions of particles being projected from the physical body. Further, some people can perceive aura as bright white light, and finally - they can perceive aura's colors.

But even here, we face problems - for you, black color might symbolize something dark, evil, dangerous, illness perhaps. For me, it's a symbol of darkness, which is positive from my point of view. This is the problem we're facing, each of you perceives colors differently. Each color has a different meaning for each person, and this meaning is based on beliefs and life experiences. Therefore, no guide can teach you how to understand aura colors if you can see them - you must learn it by yourself through practice. This is where your psychic journal kicks in. Use it to create a dictionary of aura colors and their meanings. Whenever you see a color, ask yourself a question, "what does this color means to me", and intuitively get the answer. This is how you can learn the meanings of the colors that you see.

How To See Auras

I cannot tell you if you're going to learn aura view - not everyone can. Personally, I can see aura in two ways. First, I can see it as mist like thing, particles or waving air - mainly a mix of these three things. I cannot perceive colors and here I will be honest with you. But that's just the first type - my second aura view is based on my inner psychic sight. Here, I can see shapes, symbols, colors and more. But I do this through my inner psychic eye, and not through my physical eyes.

I close my eyes or keep them open, and I do see auras as colors - even more, I can see whole energy moving throughout energy body. But I can't do this with my physical eyes, I do this "on another plane". The best way to describe it will be to say that it's like imagining an orange with your eyes open or closed - you can "see" it, but not with too many details. It's like image upon image. Like it would be my inner eye that was perceiving auras and energies. So I will teach you both techniques of aura view - the classic one, and my own.

Aura View Tutorials

Technique #1

We will start with classic technique. What you need is an object, living things works best - it might be a plant of some sort, with no flowers, just green leafs. Then you need some black background, in front of which you will place the plant. Finally, you need a candle - you can see auras in many places, but for learning purposes, we're going to prepare special "lab". Place the plant before dark background, and the candle behind you. You will be sitting between burning candle and plant, and behind plant, there will be the background. Look at the image below for references.

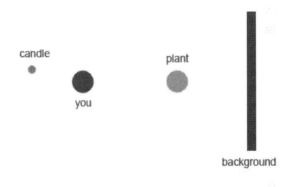

Illustration 4: Where things belong

Black background work bests for beginners, and they make aura view simpler. Turn off the light, and let only candle burning. Relax, and take few deep breaths. Count down from 0 to 10, ground and center. Now you can get to work. Focus on the plant - but don't look directly at the plant, rather focus on point few inches from actual leafs - look at another image for references.

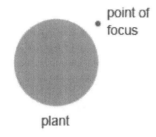

Illustration 5: Look at small dot

Start focusing - try to perceive the mist, or particles, or waving air, or light or colors - anything that seems to be a little bit extraordinary and out of place. If you can see something like the above, then it's aura. If you can't see anything after few minutes, just take another few minutes of break. There's no need to grow tired.

Some people can see aura almost instantly. Others need to take few minutes, or few sessions for a week or two; others require months; others won't be able to see aura at all. It's random ability in my opinion, but if you can't see aura, don't worry - I'm sure you're gifted in other psychic skills. And yes, you can blink. If you do see aura, all you have to do is to keep practising, and that's all. See how simple it is?

Technique #2

Now we're moving to second technique that I'm using, the technique, in which I do not see energies with my physical eye, but rather through my inner psychic sight. Repeat all the steps like in previous techniques, but this time, we don't need either the background nor any candle. Put a plant in front of you, turn off the light, relax - ground and center, count from 0 to 10 and close your eyes. Look at the plant - yes, with eyes closed for now. And try to see the plant with your inner eyes. Look for any weird shapes - blackness, whiteness or even colors. If you can't see anything, visualize the plant, and after you do this, leave it to be, just let go the control over your visualization. Perceive as what you have visualized changes - let it change freely - notice all colors and shapes, anything extraordinary. And that's all. Even so, you still have to figure out which colors represents what kind of energies.

Second technique is hard to perform by most people, because so far I was unable to find way good enough to explain how all of this looks like. But if you can see shapes and colors with eyes closed, then I believe you get the point. All of this is about visualizing first, and then letting go of control. Your inner sight should kick in.

Both techniques can be expanded further - to nonliving objects like furniture, or whole rooms, and animals and people. Energies are everywhere, so you can practice aura view everywhere. Anyway, you now know how to perceive auras through your inner sight. If you can't notice anything on the plant, then find yourself a guinea pig, a person to scan. If you're scanning the person, you can also look for energetic problems in the person's energy body and vital organs; and you can also observe chakras. All you have to do, is to intend to see the chakras, and they should become visible to you. If it doesn't work, then visualize chakras on the person, and let go of control, your psychic sight should take control. 'Scanning', in this case, is another form of aura view, but this time you're also looking for additional psychic impressions. It's like psychic reading, in which you do not depend on visual data only, but you allow your intuition to give you additional information about a person's character etc.

Physically, try to perceive auras on naked body - otherwise, you might see aura of clothes, or you might not be able to see it at all - it's because even if objects do have some slight auras, when in contact with a physical body, only living energies can be perceived, and clothes might hide any visual data from you. This is not the case when it comes to my technique as I've noticed.

A word of warning. When you're observing aura of any living or nonliving being or object, remember to break the link. Your aura perception is like an active sonar, and subconsciously, you create links between you and people or animals or objects. Through these links, you can pick up energies and emotions of these people, or they can pick up your energies and emotions. To make sure this won't happen, you always have to break links. To do so, just think "I'm breaking the link between me and … right now" - that's all. Your intention is everything you need here.

Make a note in your journal
Which technique proved to work better? Have you seen the aura at all? If yes, then how did it looked like? If you haven't seen the aura, do you believe you need more time, or should you move on and skip this talent?

Psychic Reading

One of the most popular skills within extra-sensory perception category is psychic reading - as you probably know, there are many people out there, psychics, who gives psychic readings - gives advices, discuss health problems, or discuss your personality or relationships. You can give such psychic reading yourself, because it's not very difficult skill. All you need is a bit of knowledge and proper technique. In this section, you will learn about filters, active and passive scanning, and linking. Finally, I will guide you through psychic reading in a short tutorial.

Preparation For Service

Discussing psychic readings is a perfect opportunity to mention some important things you need to know in order to perform any kind of psychic service, whether it will be psychic reading, chakra reading, psychic healing, psychometry, aura view, and things like that. There are some safety issues you need to keep in your mind. To perform a service without it is recklessness.

By the service, I understand some form of psychic work. Because it's psychic work, it might attract different entities, and different energies. You connect with the other person through psychic means, so different emotions or energies might be transferred from you to that person, and from that person to you. That is why, for one, a person that performs psychic service should really work with his or hers mind. Don't forget about psychic and spiritual growth even if you have learned some abilities. Continuous work with yourself ensures that each time, less and less negative things will be transferred to your 'customer'.

Also, when you and your 'customer' are connected, then different things might be transferred to you, as well. Concerns, worries, negative emotions, and things like that. That's why it's important to remember about the safety rules.

First, remember to light a candle each time you perform some kind of psychic work. Fire is known as etheric eraser. It draws negative energies in and burns them. Having a source of open fire is also useful when you wish to burn energies consciously. Through energy work, you can grab the energies, and cast them into the flames, then cut yourself from them by making a sign of a big X in the air, while pointing to the candle, and intending to cut yourself from the energies you just cast. It's really simple, and it doesn't require any visualization or complex energy work. You have an intend, you grab the energies with your hands, and you cast them into the candle flame.

Before psychic work, wash your hands in a stream of water. While doing so, keep an intend to wash your hands from negative energies in your mind. Perform the same task after any psychic work. If you don't have access to water, then at least use the candle flame. Hover your palms above the candle flame for few seconds.

Prepare the room, in which yo will perform the psychic work. Cleanse it by burning an incense inside. Room can be cleansed through different methods. Incense is one thing. You can also sit down in the middle of the room, and visualize the entire room being filled with bright, white light. Intend all the negative energies to be cleansed. It's a simple technique, but very effective. You should cleanse the room before and after psychic work.

After any psychic work that is somehow related to connecting with something: object, entity or person, you have to cut yourself off the target. You can do this by visualizing a link being broken, or by simple intend to cut yourself off. It's important, because this way, you won't exchange energy with your target anymore. I will discuss linking in details in just few minutes.

Finally, after psychic work, you can perform a ritual bath or ritual shower. It's not very "magical", so don't worry. It's like normal bath or shower, but you intend the water to wash you from all negative energies. So, there's no need for soap at all, just water. Of course, you can mix normal bath or shower with ritual cleansing process.

When these simple things are done, you're ready to perform the service.

It's not as you need to make all the necessary preparation before the service. Sometimes, I do quick scans and reads, or quick Reiki sessions. It's OK to do so, as long as you will be able to cleanse yourself after such short psychic work. You have to be prepared always. You can always find some kind of fire, or water, or at least incense smoke to cleanse yourself. And if you can't, then grounding and energy shower will be your best friend.

You should perform preparation before any practice session, as well. Your psychic development is psychic work, too. While you don't have to wash your hands all the time, grounding and burning a candle are wise things to do.

Energy Shower Techniques

I've mentioned energy shower earlier. It's a simple technique that can be performed before and after psychic work or practice. First, sit or stand, with your eyes either opened or closed. Inhale deeply. Then, visualize a bright, white, almost pearl, spiritual light flowing from above, and filling you from the inside out, cleansing you from negative energies. After few seconds, you're done with this simple technique.

Filters

The very first thing you need to learn about in order to give psychic reading is called a filter. In simple words, filters are special thoughts and process of management of these thoughts, that you can use to filter information you're gaining through psychic means.

There is a simple way to show you what filters are. Have you seen the Predator movie? If yes, can you remember the "sight filters" Predator had, which allowed him to see things human were not able to see? He had filters for temperature, infra-red, "alien-sight" and more, and he was able to change the filter to see different things whenever he wanted. The very same thing applies to filters. They can be use to see one thing, and ignore another.

We need an example to explain filters. Therefore, imagine a psychic trying to acquire specific information about a person, let's say "does this person likes me?" He will use his scanning abilities to find out this specific information, if the person likes or dislikes him. But will he be able to pick up other information such us: is she aggressive, sad, troubled, scared, happy? I wouldn't say so as long as he's focused on this single question "does this person likes me". And that how filters works. You focus on acquiring specific information, and ignoring everything else.

We're scanning other person looking for specific information. We're putting this "filter" inside our mind, and it picks up only the information we're looking for, while and hiding all other information away, so it can't reach us. This way, we can focus on acquiring specific information via psychic means without being overwhelmed by the amount of psychic impressions.

These filters can be created consciously, and they are being consciously created every time when we're scanning for something specific. With time and experience, a set of basic filters is created which is making use of them even easier.

Active And Passive Scanning

Scanning is a process of using psychic energies to acquire information. There are two types of scanning - passive and active.

Passive scanning is simple - energy is already there, surrounding us all the time, and it carries information which you can pick up if you will focus enough. How to pick up this information? You can use the same way to acquire information via passive scanning as you can acquire them using active scanning - with psychic reading technique. The difference is simple: in passive scanning, you do not use your own energy to link to the other person and draw information, instead you just focus on performing psychic reading when you have no connection to specific energies, you're just picking up energies that already surround you.

In case of active scanning, visualize yourself as sonar - you send your psychic energy away to the specific target. The purpose of this energy is to gather specific information, and come back to you, so you can read the information that has been collected. Practice now with these two simple exercises.

How To Scan The Area In Passive Way

Close your eyes, center and relax (you do remember what centering is, don't you?). Ask a control question - for example "is this room charged with dark or light energies, negative or positive?" - wait for images, sounds and feelings to pop up into your head. The first information you'll receive is the answer to the question, and that's what passive scanning is.

How To Scan An Object In Active Way

Now let's practice active scanning. Choose an object to test that skill, for example, a painting on the wall. Again, close your eyes, center and relax. Now send the energy from your Lower Tan T'ien through primary channel into the solar plexus, from which radiate a pulse or a stream of the psychic energy into the painting. If it's a pulse, program it gather answer to a simple question "does this painting store positive or negative energies" and then to return to you - when the pulse is programmed, simple send it away. If you decide to send a stream of energy, then first send it and then ask the question. Once again, the first thought, image, sound or feeling that will appear in your head is the answer to your question.

Now you know two ways to scan the area or object or even people - which you will use soon enough to perform a psychic reading. But first you have to learn how to link.

Linking

Linking is an important sub-skill in psychics. It can be used for psychic readings, telepathy, empathy and psychometry. It's often compared to superheroes utility belts. In order to link, you have to use energy manipulation skills to create something like a rope between you and your target. In case of psychic reading, the target will be the person you're reading. The simplest way to link is to visualize this rope made of psychic energy being created between you and the target. You might have already linked yourself to the painting on the wall from the previous exercise, but if you decided to pulse then, don't worry, you will learn now how to link anyway. Because we focus strongly on New Energy Ways, we're going to use the same technique which we used for creation of a psiball, to create a link.

So sit down with your training partner or even some object, for example, that painting I have mentioned, and begun moving the energy from your Lower Tan T'ien up to your chest and then to your solar plexus. From them, let it radiate out of you, building the link to the solar plexus of your friend. Just do this for few minutes and you're done. If you have no problems with creating psiballs, then linking won't be difficult at all. Just remember about one important thing - every time you create a link, you have to break it after you're done with what you're doing. For example, if you've created a link to give a psychic reading to someone, after the reading you have to break the link by one of the following methods:

- Visualize the link breaking and disappearing.
- Or just intend to break the link. Your intention is very powerful psychic tool.

Remember the energy follow thoughts. This is important for the good of both you and your partner.

Make a note in your journal
Have you felt the link? Did it cause any changes in mood or emotions? Have you successfully broke the link?

Psychic Development In Short Steps

At the beginning of this book, when I was discussing common misconceptions about psychics, I have mentioned about the fact that every psychic perceives things differently, based on his or hers psychic perception filters. I want to mention it again, this time to teach you important lesson. You see - I can teach you how to see things. But I cannot teach you how to understand them, or how to interpret them. Even when you will learn how to use different psychic techniques, your perception will be still yours. The only way you can learn how to understand things you see is to practice.

First, you work with your mind in order to deal with negative thought patterns. You develop your chakras, and you improve your energetics. In result, you awake your intuition. Then, you learn different techniques of psychic perception, and you start to notice different symbols, colors, scenes etc. The point is to use your intuition to learn what does the symbols and colors and scenes means. Everything else is just practice, practice, practice.

It's like practicing martial art. Your teacher can explain you the moves, but if you won't practice, your muscles and your brain won't learn, and you will have only yourself to blame. I'm teaching you what to do, but you need to be doing what I teach you in order to get better and better.

When you start your ESP practice, you will start to receive different messages: images, symbols, scenes, events, sounds, songs, different forms of psychic impressions. Remember to keep a journal of your perception, draw and describe the symbols you see. And when you see them, or hear them, or just know them, yet you do not understand what these symbolic images means, ask yourself a question: "what does this symbol means to me"? Or "what does this color means to me"? Psychic perception is subjective, and only you can define the things you see. Through practice, you can create a dictionary of your own psychic symbols and their meanings. That's why I never write down what does specific colors seen during a reading means, nor I explain different symbols. I can only tell you – ask yourself what does it means, the thing that you see. And the answer will come to you through your intuition. And with time and practice, you will be giving very accurate psychic readings.

Psychic Reading How-to

Phone or TV psychics, they all give psychic readings, some for free and some for money. They often claim this is the gift that can not be learned, but in reality everyone can give psychic reading as long as he or she will stick to some basic rules. First is that one need to develop energy system and open chakras. So when you're practicing New Energy Ways for few months now, you can learn the famous skill.

First you need a person to give the reading to. When your partner (or guinea pig) is ready, both of you should relax. The person you're giving the reading to might either hold still, or ask a specific question you will try to answer. In both cases, the reading looks the same, as follows.

Center

First, you have to center yourself (again), it means you have to focus. You can do this by focusing on the center of your head – a little point in the very middle of your brain. Focus there helps you get rid of emotions and expectations. Just keep your consciousness there at all time, and you will find it helpful to perceive more information than without centring. When you're centered, it's time to get to work!

Link

You have to connect with the person you're doing a reading for. Use the technique you've learned earlier, and link to this person - use your energy manipulation skills and visualization to visualize and create a rope made of psychic energy, between you and that other person.

Ask the question

You are now linked with the other person. Whether you're giving a reading for someone or for yourself (because you can give a reading for yourself, just like you scanned passively), you have a question, something to ask about. Below are some questions as examples:

- What should I do now?
- Will I find a better job soon?
- Does this girl likes me?
- Is Jimmy all right?
- Am I all right?

Different types of questions can be asked. It is you who asks the questions to "your psychic-self". So, if your 'customer' asked for something, then you have to repeat the question in your thoughts. When question is asked, here is where the fun begins.

Get the impression

Now, while still centered, pay attention to everything you perceive. You can get different types of psychic impressions as follows:

- **Image** – or even whole scenes, some of them might be totally abstract, some might be memories from the past (also different kinds – you can remember having a dinner, listening to music, seeing someone, playing a computer game or watching a movie). Keep focused on things you see. This is called clairvoyance - seeing things via psychic means. You might see things clearly just like you see this text now, but more likely you will

see things just like visualizing the kitchen from one of the exercises previously mentioned in this book - so don't worry if you can't see things clearly, that's perfectly normal.
- **Voice** – just like you speak words in your mind you can hear "voice" telling you something. This is called clairaudience. You won't hear real voices of course, more like a thought that is not yours - this is normal. Hearing "real" voices isn't, but it might happen if you will become skilled psychic one day.
- **Music** – this is another form of clairaudience, after asking the question you can hear music in your head, meaning a tune can literally pop up into your mind. Again, you won't here it literally, it will be like a thought in your mind.
- **Instant knowing** – finally, you can just know things. This can't be really described, as you have to experience it and understand on your own. Generally, you just know.

Start asking questions

After you get the first impression, you're getting into active part of psychic reading. Never wait for other impressions to appear after first one, because in order to do so, you need to ask a new question. This is what I call "active psychic reading" - it's all about being active. So when you got the first impression, as another question about it. Let me give you an example. Someone asked you "who is my best friend?". You asked yourself "who is this person's best friend?" and received an impression of a cat, so you can ask next "is it a cat that is this person's best friend?", and you might get an impression of a crowd applauding you which is a positive answer to that question. Then you can ask further:

- How old is this cat?
- What color this cat is?
- Is this cat black?

New impression, another question, keep the ball rolling, and you will be surprised how many information you can acquire during such psychic reading. That's what it's all about, asking questions and waiting for answers - psychic impressions.

Continue asking questions until you're done - either if you believe you can't pick up anything else, your your partner or client received the answer that satisfy him or her.

Break the link

Finally, after the reading remember to break the link, by visualizing the energy connection breaking and disappearing.

If You Can't Pick Up Anything

You might not be able to read a person, sometimes. Don't worry, it's quite normal. It happened to me, it happens to many psychics if not to all of them. Some people just can be read - because they're closed or blocked, shy, or they have psychic shielding in use. Therefore, don't worry if you can't pick up any information, or you stuck during a pretty successful reading - be honest and admit you can't read your partner. There's no way to overcome that except trying to acquire information by force, using aggressive methods of active scanning, which might be considered to be psychic attack.

Remember – only a fake psychic says that he's always accurate, and he never makes mistakes.

Make a note in your journal

Have you picked something up? What kind of information you managed to pick up? How did you perceived them? As images, sounds or something else? Were there parts of your memories, were they familiar? What unusual experiences can you recall? Were the information you picked up accurate?

It's All About Trust

In reality, psychic reading is all about trust – trust for your own mind. When performing psychic reading, you will receive a lot of psychic impressions. All you have to do is to pay attention to them, and trust your mind, trust that you're doing it right, and the information you receive is correct. If you won't trust your feelings and the impressions you get, a psychic reading will not give you anything.

Divination Systems

A lot of psychics uses divination tools such as Tarot cards or Norse runes to give psychic readings. Personally, I used to work with Norse runes, but it doesn't mean everyone should use one of such tools for additional psychic work. So why some psychics prefer them?

Tools like tarot cards or runes are a way to connect ourselves with our subconscious mind - our higher self as some call it. They are the tool of focus, and tool of translating information from subconscious to our conscious self. With them, it's possible to give even more accurate psychic readings. But it's not the reason why some psychics use cards or runes. Those who do this are beginners who are not well tuned into their inner thoughts and intuition - that piece of psychic mind. So they require additional tools. And with time, they can't help themselves and they stick with using tarot or Runes.

Therefore, is it worth it? Should you choose additional tool for psychic readings? If you believe that accurate psychic readings are something you wish to learn for whatever reason there might be, then yes - experiment with runes, tarot, classic cards or I Ching or any other divination system. If you believe such tools work well with you, then use them. If you think you don't like them, don't use them. It's that simple.

And if you have been using additional tools for years, and now you want to get rid of them and become "pure" psychic, as I call it, then put the tools away, and slowly learn to listen to your inner self - that is what you've been doing all over the time, just now you're out of the tools. Meditation and practice are the only keys here. And the choice is all yours.

Psychometry

Psychometry is a common ability best know from TV shows, where a psychic touches some physical object like a photo and describes what he sees or sense. In reality, the ability isn't really different from psychic reading, but this time instead of reading a person, we're reading an object.

How Does Psychometry Works?

Psychic energies are everywhere, in every living being and object. The object, whether it's a home item such as family photo or kitchen knife, or an old castle wall, acquire psychic energies that are being emitted from people and events, it's called with the term of psychic imprint. Such imprint might remain in the object forever and then be read by a skilled psychic, or it can manifest itself as a residual haunting (people used to call it ghosts). It's all based on psychic energies that can carry information as psychic impressions – the reader just know how to filter and pick this information up.

Psychometry is a skill that can be used to read different objects, here are some examples:

- **Photos** – made of paper, with a frame, they're often related to people and family. They can contain a lot of emotional and relationship information, about people or animals, or even other objects that have been photographed.
- **Walls** – especially often in old buildings, they gather residual energies of the past, and they can inform you about the events of the past. Don't hesitate to touch the wall in order to do a reading.
- **Furniture** – typical home objects, especially armchairs can give you a lot of information about the person that used to sit there.
- **Toys** – when dealing with child problems, their toys can contain vital information about emotional and mental state.

You can also read objects in the museum. Just remember, you don't have to touch the object, just link to it with psychic linking. Psychometry can give you answers to relationship problems, family and child problems, history of the locations, to events that happened there, and people who lived there. It's a useful skill when doing historical or archaeological research, performing a paranormal investigation, or even crime investigation, looking for missing people and even more. As you can see, psychometry is a useful skill to learn. And you're about to learn it now.

How To Perform Psychometry

What you need is an object of some sort, for now I would suggest something from your home, an item that belongs to a member of your family or if you can't find such thing, an item that belongs to your friend maybe. Just make sure it's nothing that belongs to you because then you already know the object and you wont' read anything you wouldn't already know. The item you choose should be well known to the owner, so he can confirm or deny your psychic findings. Let's get to work.

- **Center** – As always, you have to center yourself first. It's the very same skill as centring mentioned many times in this book already so you know what to do.
- **Warm up** – Next, use the New Energy Ways and Mobile Body Awareness to warm up the hand which you will use for this psychometry session. Personally I'm using my left hand even if it's not my dominant hand, because it's more sensitive to psychic energy. When using Mobile Body Awareness, just move the energy with brushing and circling actions.
- **Link** – Now that you're warmed up, it is time to use your energy manipulation skills to create a link between you and the object. Pick the object up with your hand and while holding it, imagine a link made of psychic energy being created, connecting your palm and the object itself together. You already know how to link, so it should be easy.
- **Shift awareness** - It's time for you to shift your awareness with Mobile Body Awareness. Focus completely on your physical hand, and do not think about anything else. Feel only your hand for now, and the energy moving there. Basic shifting awareness is just changing the point of focus of your consciousness.

Now, while sensing your physical hand, shift awareness to the object you're holding – feel it as it would be a physical part of your body. When you're done, you have successfully shift your awareness, and you can begin the reading.

- **Read the object** – As I said before, psychometry isn't very different from classic psychic readings. You have to remember about few things. While holding the object and shifting your awareness to it, stay centered and ask the question: how does the item feels like. Try to see the picture, or hear a sound, or feel something – interpret the impressions you receive via psychic means. Then ask another question and pay attention to new impressions. And that's how it works. In reality, you can use all the knowledge about psychic readings in case of psychometry.
- **Break the link** - When you're done, and you believe you can't read anything else, or the answer has been given, remember to break the link, so you won't become connected with the object for a longer time that is required.

Now you know how to perform psychometry. You might want to touch the object which you're reading, because it's making stronger connection (link) with it. When you're done with reading, ask the owner about your findings, let him confirm or deny the impressions you received.

What Kind Of Information Can You Pick Up?

Almost anything can be picked up via psychic means during psychometry session – the emotions of the item's owner, the physical condition of this person, the events that happened around this object, circumstances that lead to the events. You can hear sounds, see pictures and whole scenes, know things and get physical and emotional feelings. Anything that can be picked up psychically and emotionally by using normal five senses, can be picked up with psychometry, as well.

Make a note in your journal

Have you picked up any information? How did you perceive them? Were they similar to information picked up during human-to-human psychic reading, or were they different perhaps? Was it difficult to pick information from in-animated objects?

Telepathy

Telepathy is a skill that allows people to communicate over short and long distances with the use of no verbal means, using only psychic abilities. Although I have never met with proofs that it's possible to communicate word-by-word (some people refer to it as mind reading), it's possible to learn telepathy - if you will understand how it looks like.

Telepathy is about consciously picking up extra-sensory perception - psychic impressions that you should already know well enough. For example, if your friend is transmitting the color red, you got impressions that tell you that it's color read - for example you might see images of many red objects you have encountered in your life. And that's how you should perceive this skill.

I'm going to provide you with basic telepathy tutorial. To perform the following exercises, you need practice partner. If you have it already, let's get to work.

Prepare a room for the training purpose. Create some barrier between you and your partner - some wall made of cardboard will be enough. Now you need to prepare a set of color pieces of paper - they will be your tool of focus. Finally, when everything is ready, we can move further.

- **Sender** - close your eyes, relax, ground and center. Focus on first color of your choice, and start sending - do this, by intending to transmit information about the color to your partner. Visualize the color in your mind, and use energy manipulation to send short pings of energy - like small balls of psychic impressions. Target them to your partner, and keep the intend for them to transfer information.
- **Receiver** - relax, ground and center. With eyes closed, start perceiving information - look for clues, observe images closely - what can you see? Objects, people? The color should reach you as memory images, because that's how your brain works. So pay attention to any impressions you're receiving.

When the color is guessed correctly, move on to another one. Keep the "score" in some notebook. And basically that's it - focus on information, recall some images and familiar things related to this information, and ping it. That's whole philosophy. Later, you can experiment with numbers, then letters and feelings.

Art of Remote Viewing

During the Cold War, Russians were experimenting with different psychic abilities and their application for dark military purposes - their primary areas of focus were telepathy and telekinesis, but they also developed interesting system of energy manipulation. Due to spy activity, government of United States became aware of the Soviet research, and decided to start their own experiments. Department of Defense, working with Stanford Research Institute, began research into so called Remote Viewing - the ability to perceive events, people and objects over great distances, with no use of any ordinary physical senses. Years later, small research turned into Stargate Program, and then - everything stopped. Soviet Union was no more but does the research into military applications of psychic abilities really stopped? Well, that we do not know.

What we know is that thanks to participants of that research, we have access to complete manuals on CRV – so called Controlled Remote Viewing. Even if whole manuals and protocols for remote viewing process would cause this book to go for 500 pages, it's possible to present you with ultimate basics that will allow you to experiment and practice remote viewing by your own.

By now, you should have nicely developed energy body, and quite a lot of experience in practical psychic abilities. All you need to do now is to learn the theory, basic protocols, and start your development in another psychic field.

Theory

Before we proceed to practical remote viewing, it's always good to learn more about theory of this phenomena. You have already learned that psychic abilities work because of psychic energies flowing around. The energies transfer information, and interact with the physical world. It's the basic theory that is enough for most psychic abilities to work and it can be utilized when it comes to remote viewing too.

But you should also learn about Matrix theory. What is the Matrix? Imagine that it's a field of psychic energies, parallel to our own reality, that stores are information that ever were, are or will be – here and now. Using thing called "coordinates", a psychic – in this case called remote viewer – is able to plug himself into the Matrix, and acquire specific information.

And that's the theory – coordinates point the viewer to a specific set of information located on the Matrix. And you don't even have to navigate throughout it, you don't even have to know how it's possible for coordinates to work. All you need to keep in mind is that coordinates work, and simple by thinking about them, you are plugging into the information that is already there. Your job is to learn how to receive information.

Different Types Of Remote Viewing

Actually, remote viewing is just another form of clairvoyance – it's not really a skill by itself, rather a set or specific protocols that help you utilize other psychic perception to accomplish a specific task such as locating an object, or person, or finding out as much as you can about a specific location. So do not threat it as yet another psychic talent, rather a set of guidelines that help you accomplish a specific task.

Following this way of thinking, in this book you will learn about two protocols for successful remote viewing. There will be only one tutorial, and your job will be to replace "coordinates" with "beacon" or vice versa. Don't worry if you don't know what does it mean, I will explain everything as we proceed. So here are these two protocols.

Outbound Remote Viewing

Outbound remote viewing takes place, where a person is dispatched to a specific location, and remote viewer's job is to perceive that location. In this case, the person that is called the "beacon" acts as coordinates for the whole procedure. There's no big philosophy for this protocol. The beacon just get to the location, stands or sits there for a specific amount of time, and then leaves. Everything else is the viewer's job.

Coordinated Remote Viewing

In case of coordinated remote viewing, there is no beacon – but there are coordinates. Coordinates looks like this: 21:81, or 21:82:21:76 or even abcd – there's no guideline here. A person must first assign the coordinates. Let's say there is that nice lake near Zywiec, Poland – it's small town near my home village. You have no idea where it is, but it doesn't matter – there is a lake there. Now I assign coordinates to it – 81:42. That's is – those are coordinates for the lake near Zywiec town in Poland.

I assigned coordinates simple by thinking about that particular lake, and assigning few digits to it. The information has been recorded on the Matrix, now all the viewer must do, is to think about these coordinates, think of the location they represent, and perceive the information.

There is a problem here – let's say two people on the world assign the same coordinates for two different places. Which one will you pick up? First, that's why I encourage creation or longer coordinates that are more difficult to accidental repeat themselves. Second, that's the great part of remote viewing. If you're searching for "this" coordinates, you will see only one site assigned to them – even if there are two ab:ab coordinates pointing different location, first ab:ab will only point to "its own" location, while the second ab:ab will point "its own" location. They can't interfere with each other, so don't worry.

Analytical Overlay

Analytical Overlay, in short A.O.L., is a situation when thoughts and ideas cross-wire themselves, and you become confused. It's a common problem in psychic phenomena, when you can't pick up which information is right, and which isn't. When you receive information, the brain automatically looks for references in memory banks – for example, if I say "yellow", your brain will look for yellow things like banana, for example, or yellow carpet. We can't stop it, and because of this, when in reality, remote viewer perceives yellow car, he might think it's yellow banana – why the case of this perception is the color itself. If I see something that is long, yellow and cylindrical, I may believe it to be a pencil, but in reality, it is a garbage can.

Scribbling Technique

There is a way out of this problem called "scribbling". What you need is a paper and something to draw. When you receive information, you can draw what you see, or use lines to mark things – draw one line for adjective, and two lines for noun. When they come to you together, simple crosses the lines together. The point is to connect physical actions with mental activity and information you're receiving. That way – your brain understand you have received the information, and it doesn't have to throw it at you again, "both of you" can move on.

Keep the above technique in mind – it will become your most important tool in whole remote viewing procedure.

Remote Viewing Tutorial

The most important step in remote viewing is to choose the protocol – it's all up to you if you will decide to use coordinates, or the beacon. First, someone – second person, should become a beacon and more to a specific location you know nothing about (that's an important thing, you can't know the target; otherwise, RV session will not be accurate). Or if you decide for Coordinate RV, that person should choose the location, and assign coordinates – using the method I already described. When the coordinates are set, or the beacon is on the site, we're getting to work.

Create proper room for RV session – make sure it's clean – the best room would be empty, with a single chair and table, free of outside noises and light, with covered windows. Peaceful and quiet, it will be the place where you can focus. Prepare a paper and something to write, and sit down. It's time to relax your mind.

There are few methods of relaxation – close your eyes, and breath deeply. Count down from 30 to 0. Or from 0 to 30, using the method I described earlier in meditation exercise. Or tense or relax your muscles, one by one. Your mind must be at peace, and you must be relaxed – otherwise, whole RV might not work at all. When you're relaxed, you can move on.

Take the pencil (or any other tool you're using for writing) and close your eyes. Relaxed, star perceiving – think of the coordinates, or the beacon – keep an intend of perceiving the location. You might receive images, thoughts, sounds, even smells. You will fall under attack of different information, but don't worry – keep relaxing, and seek smaller bits of information. Stick to adjectives, and leave the nouns for later. If you see something that is red, don't jump to a conclusion that it's a red car – say "rectangular red shape" and move on. It's possible to be transferred to the location – it's called remote presence – you're not really "there", just your consciousness is, so you have nothing to worry about.

Collect as much information as possible before jumping to conclusions. The more details you get, the greater the possibility is that you will "hit the target". How so? Well, if I think about rectangular red shape, directly connected to long black line, and four black circles, when I got the "feel" of speed, or momentum, I can't think of anything else than red car on the street. You got the point, don't you? Basically – just like in case of psychic readings it's all based on experience and interpretation. The more details you have and the more experience you have, the greater the possibility is you will be able to hit your targets with great accuracy.

And that's all – such RV session might take few minutes, or 30 minutes, or an hour, or few hours – the more time you spend during such session, the more details you get. When you're finally done with perceiving, if you have the way of confirming your findings, do this.

Confirming Findings and Practice Sessions

How can you confirm your findings? Simple by visiting the location. At first it will be great to practice with familiar places or objects. Ask your friend to collect a bunch of photos of different places, objects or people. Ask him not to show the photos to you, but rather assign coordinates to them carefully. Then you'll just run RV session on each image, and ask your friend to show you that particular photo – this way, you will be able to confirm your minds, and learn how your mind perceives different things. That will further improve your remote viewing skills. You can move the exercises further, and try Outbounded protocols, or you can assign coordinates to physical locations in your town.

How Can Remote Viewing Be Used

Finally, why should you learn remote viewing? Imagine that someone is lost – a person, good friend of yours, or little girl from the neighborhood. Remote Viewing can be used here, to locate here – a photo would be needed, so you could look at the face of missing person, because you will use Outbounding protocol – the missing person will be the beacon, and you will try to perceive surrounding area to locate where he or she might be. Remote Viewing can be also used to locate missing objects. In such case, we will use Coordinated protocol. Finding out things, learning more about locations you're going to visit, acquiring information of a different sort – there are many possibilities you can explore.

Few additional notes and tips for remote viewing:

1. Keep A.O.L. in mind – try to avoid nouns, they're treacherous.
2. "Hire a monitor" - ask someone to help you out by monitoring whole RV session – use camcorders and voice recorders to record RV procedures. It's especially important when searching for lost objects or people – your monitor might be able to interpret data you're picking up better, and this results in success.

When assigning coordinates, the person doing this should also be relaxed. The calmer the mind is, the more accurate coordinates will be.

Make a note in your journal

How did you perceive information that you were receiving? How accurate were you? Have you experienced anything unusual during remote viewing session?

Precognition and Dreams

With your psychic abilities slowly developing, you may notice that you can remember more and more dreams. And some of them might turn out to be precognitive dreams. Precognition is a psychic ability to perceive the future events, mainly in a short period of time counting from "here and now". It's a good idea to start a dreams journal and write down all the dreams you remember at the moment you wake up, because the longer you are awake, the less of your dreams you remember. Either get a notebook and place it near your bed, or make sure your laptop will be there when you wake up.

Write down your dreams, and return to your previous entries from time to time, maybe you will suddenly discover that some of your dreams came true? I can remember that one day I was going through my dreams journal, and I stumbled upon to a dream I had somewhere in May of 2007. In the dream, I saw a chart, an economical graph of some kind that was going down. I knew it was something related to the economy and money, but I didn't know exactly what does the dream meant. About 1.5 year later I was reading through my journal, and I saw this dream. I already knew it was related to the global economic crisis that we faced in years 2007-2009. A truly fascinating experience, I have to admit.

By now, you might already have few journals: a primary one; core images list; affirmations journal; and now your dreams journal. It's better writing them down separately, because it's much easier to use them this way.

Empathy

Empathy probably is the most popular skill when it comes to psychic development. It's literally sensing emotions and physical condition of people like they would be your own. I do have tons of examples for this ability: I can sense when people are angry, tired, sad, when they're in pain both physical and emotional, or ill. This ability can be controlled by simple shields mentioned few pages earlier. But how to develop the empathic abilities? You don't have to, because this skill will come to you with time. After few months of energy work, you might start noticing that you can sense emotions that aren't really yours, and that they're gone as soon as you set up a shielding around you. Sometimes it's referred to as cursed gift, and I have an example to explain why.

I was standing in the queue, and in front of me was an older woman with her son, about 30 years. But there was something odd about him, soon I realized he was mentally handicapped. As soon as I realized this, I unconsciously linked with the woman and picked up emotions I can feel for this day - her fear for what will happen to her son when she will pass away, her pain over her son life. I had to control myself; otherwise it would look weird for me to start crying in the queue in chemists store.

Remember to use psychic shielding and grounding when you suffer from emotions of others, and to center, as well. The best way to deal with empathic feelings is to analyze your sensations and emotions, and recognize which of them are yours, and which aren't. Following the example above, I couldn't identify fear of the future of my son as my own fear, if I don't have a son, so I knew it was not my emotion. So, there's not point to worry about it. Yet, I admit, feeling emotional pain of others is... difficult, at least sometimes. I guess we just need to get over it, if shields and grounding doesn't help.

It is possible to get over negative empathic responses, but it requires many months, perhaps even years of spiritual development. Through studies of Taoist texts and Buddhist sutras, one can learn that pain and negative emotions are natural for every human being. And they come and go. Taoist and Buddhist practices teach not to attach yourself to negative feelings. And through such practice, one can be free of negative emotions forever. They will be there, still, and you will experience them. But if you won't pay attention to them, then they won't be painful. Yet, this is just an idea for you to explore, as the subject of such spiritual growth is to wide for this book to describe it.

Psychic empathy result in one more thing – overload, when you spend your time among big groups of people. Shopping centers, stadiums, concerts, clubs and such can generate a lot of aggressive energy that can drain you of positive energies, and overload your system with negative energies. Remember to ground yourself, and shield, as well. But the best way to deal with this kind of problem is to spend as little time among big groups of highly emotional people as possible.

Advanced Energy Work

"He who knows that enough is enough will always have enough."

The following tutorials are meant to teach you about very popular skills, but remember – if you haven't stick to this book's schedule for few months, you might not get any positive results with these two techniques. But as always, do not expect results, yet observe and see what will come up.

Psychic Healing

In many cases, people want to develop psychic abilities in order to heal - themselves or others. Today, in a world full of illness and diseases, cancer, AIDS and other terrible things, people keep hearing about miraculous heals. And they want to know if they can heal themselves or others in such miraculous way, too. The answer is simple, yes they can - but there's no miracle included here.

Psychic healing is something very natural - the physical body gets ill because the psychic energies flowing inside the energy system are unbalanced. Many Eastern martial arts such as Tai Chi Chuan focus on doing both physical and psychical exercises that are meant to keep the balance, and provide body with enough energy to maintain health. Don't worry about that one, because daily practice of New Energy Ways is enough to keep the energetic balance and keep yourself free of many diseases. But psychic energies won't keep you safe from each and every disease - sometimes even a simple cold might get through and nail you to bed.

If you or any other person become a victim of cold, flu, or even more complex diseases, there's a need to use psychic techniques and target healing psychic energies in order to heal the physical body. One of the Eastern practice called Reiki does that - it focuses psychic energies for healing purposes, and in some way, this is what you're going to learn right now - how to use psychic energies to heal.

What you need is a practical New Energy Ways knowledge, the ability to manipulate energies and create psiballs - with enough practice of these skills, you will be able to modify the techniques for psychic healing purposes. Make sure to practice exercises from this e-book for five months; otherwise, you might not get enough energy manipulation skills to perform psychic healing.

Now, to actual tutorial. This is another psychic technique, and this time meant to teach you how to perform a psychic healing. Let's say you have a place within a physical body that is ill. It might hurt, or might be twisted ankle, damaged liver etc.

You need to know the ill place before proceeding with this psychic healing technique. When you know what is going to be healed, we can move forward.

Warm up your hands using New Energy Ways. Use circling and brushing actions to do so, and continue warming up process for about three minutes. When you're done, place both of your hands on the body part that is going to be healed.

Center yourself, focus on the middle of your head and on the task you're going to accomplish - this task is simple, to heal the damaged body part.

Start pumping psychic energies into the person's body. Visualise the energy as green, intend it to be positive in nature. It's time for psychic programming, meaning: your intend is to heal the body part. If it's just pain, your intent will be to take away that pain. If it's something more, just have positive thoughts in your mind and know the energy you're pumping is meant to heal that specific body part.

When you pump first wave of positive energies, which should take about 3 seconds, pull out negative energies from a person's body - this specific body part to be exact. Do this for another 3 seconds and then pump another wave of positive energies, and pull out negative energies again. It's a form of psychic energy exchange. You're giving the person positive energies, while taking negative energies in return. All you need is the intend to exchange these energies, and intend to heal.

Continue this process of psychic healing for few minutes. After you're done, stop the energy exchange and ground yourself. Move negative energies towards the ground and get rid of them. That's all.

If the illness is complex, you might need few longer sessions of psychic healing. For a flu or cold, you should exchange energy from the entire body, not just single ill body part. But for taking the pain away which is the simplest way to use psychic healing, about 30 seconds will be enough to stop thinking about painkillers.

Just remember about a very important thing - no matter what you're about to heal, always consult with a doctor. You can try psychic healing, but always remember that you're not a skilled doctor of medicine, and in reality, your psychic healing can only support real healing process.

Make a note in your journal
How did it feel when you attempted psychic healing? And did it work? Have you noticed faster healing rate than normally?

Reiki

If you really want to learn psychic healing, then instead of learning pure, energetic healing, that drains your own energies, you should learn about Reiki, and become initiate to Reiki practice. It is a system of energy healing created by Mikao Usui at the beginning of XX century in Japan, and during the next hundred years, it expanded to the entire world. In order to become initiated, you need to find a teacher that will initiate you, attune you to spiritual energies of Reiki.

After initiation, you can use Reiki for both psychic healing, and your own spiritual and psychic growth. Yes, Reiki can speed up your psychic development, so it's another reason why you might be interested in Reiki initiation. But more than this, Reiki isn't draining your own energies, so psychic healing with Reiki won't leave you tired, and won't influence your emotional status. But as any form of spiritual energy, it can speed up your spiritual growth, by re-emerging negative patterns from your mind. At the same time, Reiki can help you deal with these patterns, so it's not very dangerous for your emotional health. Benefits are great, and definitely worth it.

Telekinesis

One of the most flashy psychic abilities is telekinesis - the ability to manipulate physical matter with your mind. It's also known as psychokinesis, and it's a simple skill in theory. Use psychic mind to move physical object without actually touching it. Telekinesis can be divided into two groups - micro and macro. Micro-Telekinesis is based on psychically affecting random events, such as rolling dice. Macro-Telekinesis, on the other hand, is meant to move larger objects, and it doesn't include affecting randomness.

I have to admit, telekinesis is very popular psychic ability and a lot of beginners tries to learn it first. This is where they fail to do so - it's very advanced skill at the same time, and trying to learn it as first to go doesn't show your healthy approach to psychic development. Of course, you can ignore my expert opinion and try to learn telekinesis anyway, without learning elementary skills, but I'm more than sure - you will fail.

Therefore, please keep in mind - telekinesis can't be learned if elementary skills has not been mastered first. Even so, it's hard to learn telekinesis at all - it's difficult skill that not many people posses. But who knows - maybe you're one of such people? I will be honest with you - my telekinesis experience is based solely on two spoons successfully bent after weeks of experimentation, and some experiments with psi-wheel, so the following section about telekinesis, as only section in this book, will be based mainly on theory, and my understanding of the skill - and some practical experiences to some degree.

Micro-Telekinesis

Your adventure with telekinesis you will start with learning how to throw a dice. Micro-Telekinesis is all about it - affecting random effects. It's a good way to start, and even if such skill could be used in a Casino, I can hardly find any practical use for it. But even if I believe you do not need to learn micro-telekinesis at all, I will provide short tutorial for those who would like to master this skill.

- **Prepare a dice** - classic black-and-white dice will do. Also, prepare a piece of paper and something to write. Write down digits from 1 to 100. This is the number of trials you will run during single practice session.
- **Relax your mind** - perform classic preparation, calm down, count from 1 to 30, ground and center.
- **Start throwing** - close your eyes, think of the number you want to see on the top of the dice when it stops - just think about it, keep the intend. Then simple throw the dice and wait for it to stop.

If you managed to make a "hit", and the number you wanted is on the top, then mark the trial as hit. If it's different digit, then mark it as missed. Simple run all 100 trials, and do the math - if the number of hits is over 65, then there definitely is some PSI factor included here. Yet - for some reasons no psychic ever published good tutorial for micro-telekinesis, nor any psychic development guide I ever read provides information about the subject. Therefore, even if you can play around, I encourage you to head directly to macro-telekinesis.

Macro-Telekinesis

Macro-telekinesis is all about moving bigger objects - psi-wheel, cans, dishes, even big cars. OK, skip that car thing. Although if you look around, you can find information about experiments that included movement of pretty big things, but I wouldn't really rely on it - not that it's not possible, but because it shouldn't consider you right now. I will provide you with general tutorial for movement, and then I will explain what's with the psi-wheel tool. Are you ready?

General Tutorial For Movement

Telekinesis once again is about psychic energies. But, while ESP is generally about picking up information, telekinesis can be described as use of energy manipulation for interaction with the outside world. The point is - to use psychic energies to move objects. Based on theory, experiences of others and my own experience here's the general tutorial for telekinetic movement.

- **Relax** - clear your mind, count from 1 to 30, ground and center. That procedure should be obvious by now, right?
- **Move the energy** - let's say there's an object in front of you. Keep your eyes open, and think of moving the object. "Create" that intend in your mind. Then use New Energy Ways and tactile visualization to expand your energy body from your dominant energy hand into the object - use your mobile awareness and visualization to touch the object. Continue expanding the field to the point when you will totally cover the object you want to move - like you would hold it in your grasp.

- **Move the object** - now, that your energy reached the object, focus on moving it - keep that intend and direct it onto the object. Use tactile visualization to push the object. Keep that intend for few minutes.

If it won't work, then take a break and try again. Do not try to move the object with this technique for longer than 5 minutes - take breaks often and don't give up to soon. That is the general tutorial.

Psi-Wheel How-To

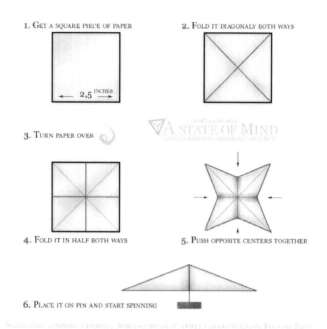

Illustration 6: Psi-Wheel step by step

We're going to test this technique on Psi-Wheel. Psi-Wheel is a tool supposedly developed by Russians during Cold War to practice telekinesis. It's also known as "paper-on-pin", because that's what it is - a star-shaped piece of paper placed on pin. Below you can see the image that will help you create that piece of tool.

The problem with psi-wheel is that it's easily moved by air - for example, if you breath on it, it will move. Or if the temperature in the room will start to increase, the hot air will ascend according to the laws of physics, and that will be enough to move psi-wheel, too. Therefore, you should place the tool under some transparent basin, jar or shade, so environmental condition won't easily moved it. Don't worry - such physical barrier shouldn't influence energy transfer between you and the object. Now we're going to move the psi-wheel.

Use the general tutorial I included earlier - relax, then extend your energy body to grasp the object, and try to spin it with intend and energy push. After few minutes without success, take a break. If it will move, try spinning it in the opposite direction. That's it!

You can practice with psi-wheel for few weeks before you will move to bigger objects. Try to experiment with empty cola cans, for example. And if you see no results, just keep trying. But keep in mind one thing - affecting material world with psychic skills is one of the hardest skills to learn - do not rely on negative results to much, if you have no success in telekinesis, focus on extra-sensory perception skills - after all, these are the primary core elements of psychic phenomena, and of course - most useful.

How To Bend Spoons

Mind-over-matter, as many people use to call this skill, is best represented by the skill of bending spoons and forks. This isn't an easy skill to learn and perform, but at the same time, it's easiest in theory. In order to bend a spoon, first grab a spoon and hold in one of your hands, the best will be to choice the dominant energy hand. Again, my dominant energy hand is my left, it sense and manipulate energies better than right hand.

Now, let's get to work. You can bend a spoon with your eyes both closed or open. Sit down and make sure you're comfortable.

- While holding the spoon within your hand, center. You should already know that centring is the most important skill for psychic work
- Now, start the energy flow. Psychic energies should flow from your Lower Tan T'ien, up to your dominant energy arm, then down the arm to your hand, and into the spoon - but that's just the beginning of the circle.
- Put an index finger of your other hand on the tip of the spoon. Continue to move the energy through that index finger, through your second hand and arm, back to the Lower Tan T'ien. When the circle is done, just keep the energy flowing back and forth through the energy circle you have just created.
- At the same time, you need to program the energy. Keep the intend of the energy making the spoon softer and softer, second by second. Continue energy work for another 3 to 5 minutes.
- Next, say aloud or just inside your mind (the best way for many is saying it aloud, really) "bend, bend, bend" - shout it if you must, you need to give a clear intend "to the spoon". Finally, you need some distraction - think about something else, for example, about that nice girlfriend you meet yesterday. When thinking about something else, keep trying the spoon - if it's getting softer, just enjoy the bending process.

If you weren't able to bend a spoon in about a minute or two since you gave it the order, stop for few minutes and try one more time the bending process from energy circle to bending the spoon. With time and practice, it will become easier and easier.

If you are unable to bend a spoon, then either your energy manipulation skills are too weak, and you need to develop them first, or you have mental blockages that disallow you to believe truly in the skill of telekinesis. In such case, you will have to work over these blockages, and re-program your mind. Or, you can seek a spoon bending workshop near you. Seeing someone actually bending a spoon can easily re-program your own mind into believing that such ability is possible. Thus, your own skills in spoon bending can awake.

Make a note in your journal
Have you managed to move any object or bend the spoon? What unusual sensations have you felt during telekinesis practice?

Know that it might take some time before you will successfully bend your first spoon. I have one last advice for you – look around in your place if there is any spoon bending workshop. Or organize a workshop by yourself, by asking someone you know could bend spoons or move objects with telekinesis. It's very popular phenomena – that when people gather together to learn telekinetic skills, and they're guided by someone who already can do things, they can do it also – right after seeing his or her skills with their own eyes. Keep that in mind – it might become a useful knowledge for your future research.

Last, But Not Least

"A journey of 1000 miles begins with a single step."

It may take time before you will get use to your training schedule, and psychic work. You already have learned everything that you really need to know if you want to become psychic. In the last chapter of this book, I provide you with additional knowledge that proves to be useful in daily psychic life. It's not mandatory, but it might come in handy. We will start with discussing pendulums and crystals in psychic work.

Pendulums And Rods

Using pendulums and rods (the process of using rods is called dowsing) is another common element by which psychics are recognized. Dowsing, often misunderstood for searching for water only, in reality is the process of searching for energy streams. It is a common believe that one requires a gift to use rods because not everyone can sense the energy being conducted by the rods into hands. But in reality, everyone have this 'gift' – just like anyone can become psychic. Using both your psychic energies and your intuition, you can quickly learn how to use pendulums and rods for your own work.

Pendulum, on the other hand, is a simple device that help you in communicating with your subconscious, or spirit guide, or higher psychic-self - you name it. A pendulum is build of two elements – a string, and a heavier object hanged on the string. It is a belief that information that you pick up using psychic means are noticed by subconscious, which is sending electric impulses causing micro-twitches in your hands, which are causing the pendulum to move. Because of this, pendulum is a way to make psychic readings easier, yet it can answer only simple questions such as these with two possible answers - yes or no. Yet, with time you can create a template for getting more complex answers.

For some, pendulums might not be easier to use (some people prefer to use other psychic means), but definitely, pendulums are not draining too much of your energies. As you already know, whenever you use psychic ability, it drains your own psychic energies. Therefore, with time, you might become tired and even unable to use your psychic skills until you recharge your batteries. Pendulums, on the other hand, do not deplete your energies, and can be used more often, and for longer periods of time. Therefore, you might want to consider learning how to use a pendulum.

There are different types of pendulums, and different types of rods. Since this is Psychic Development Simplified, I will stick to the simplest model of a pendulum, and I will skip the rods entirely, simple because I do not use them in my practice.

Getting Your Own Pendulum

Before we start using a pendulum, we have to get it first – you can buy it, or build it on your own – there's no difference, really. Actually, if someone tells you that you need to buy a professional pendulum as otherwise it won't work, he is lying, or he doesn't know what he's talking about. There is a tradition that women use their wedding rings, suspended on one of their hairs, to sway the gender of their unborn baby. A wedding ring, a piece of a mineral or crystal. Personally, at the beginning of my practice I was using an old fuse painted black, and it was working well. Of course if you can afford it, you can buy a pendulum, as it's all about object hanging in the air, at least in case of basic pendulums. Yet, I have to admit, experts in using pendulum and radionics – a branch of parapsychology that deals with pendulums and rods – says that some shapes of pendulums gives better effect for specific types of questions – in other words, some pendulums work better for searching water on a map, and other works better for searching gold in the field. How much truth there is in this, should not be your concern yet. First you have to learn how to use a pendulum.

So build your pendulum – place some kind of object on a string (not on a metal chain, please), and the pendulum is ready to be used.

How To Use A Pendulum

Pick up the pendulum – make sure you rest your arm on a table or chair or whatever, it will keep your hand steady which is very important. Hold the string between your thumb and index finger – of course you can hold it differently if you like, but this is basic "hold". You need to find your 'wave length'. To do so, follow your intuition – ask the Source (or your higher psychic self) for guidance, and listen for the answer. You should quickly learn where should you hold your string. If you're having problems with your intuitive guidance, try this: hold the pendulum at the beginning of the string, as close to the pendulum's head as possible, and ask the ask the pendulum to show you what swing will represent "yes", and what swing will be for "no" - it should start moving. If it doesn't, change your grip, hold the string a centimeter higher than before, and repeat the question. If it still doesn't move, repeat the process of changing your grip, and continue it, until the pendulum will start to swing. When it does, make a knot on the string, to mark the place where you should hold the pendulum. Now, you have found the wave length, and you're ready to use the pendulum for good.

As I said, ask the pendulum to show you the swing for answer 'yes' first, then ask the pendulum to show you the swing for answer 'no'. Remember the ways pendulum swings, as it will be important for your work. The question themselves can be asked aloud, or within your mind only.

If you want, you can create a template for answers – it's a simple piece of paper, with a circle on it, and four sections – two for "yes" answers, and two for "no". Additional templates can be sued for marking letters and digits, as well, so it could help you out with more complex questions.

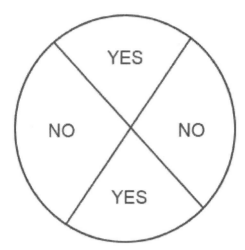

Illustration 7: Simple template for "yes" & "no" answers

Exercise With Cards

Now you know swings for both "yes" and "no", so we can use this knowledge for some fun and small experiment. Take a cards deck (usually 52 cards), shuffle them and pick up random three (3) cards, don't look at all of them, just pick up one and remember it, then put it back into your three-cards minideck and shuffle all three cards again. Put them on desk (suits on the bottom) and pick up your pendulum.

Ask a question: "does the first card from the right is my card", but instead of "my card" name your card (e.g. ace of spades), close your eyes and relax, keep the question in your mind. After few seconds open your eyes and take a look at the swing of your pendulum – if it's not moving, close your eyes again, relax and think about the question for few more seconds. Finally, you will get the answer – if your pendulum show you "no", then ask the same question about the card in the middle – if it's still not this card, then it must be third one.

You have to learn to trust the movements of your pendulum – if it's moving, then it's moving correctly. Keep practising this and you will find your results interesting. Pendulum can be used to guess things, find the right answer or path, find missing objects using a map or just give basic psychic readings.

During the war in Vietnam, US army was using experts in pendling to find secret tunnels of the Viet Cong. And today, pendling is very popular tool of archaeological exploration, even if not many people admit it. Psychics with pendulum are searching for abandoned archaeological sites all over the world. It's quite complex subject, but if you would like to explore it further, let me tell you this. All you need to find lost places, people or objects with pendulum, is a simple map. Hover the pendulum over the map, ask questions and wait for answers. You can even move the pendulum all over the map and wait for it to swing. That's it! Keep using your pendulum as often as possible, and design your own exercises to analyze your results. And have fun!

Make a note in your journal

How did the pendulum feel? Did you enjoy the movement? Did it worked at all? And what where the results of the above exercises? How did you felt? Any weird sensations, or emotions? Do you enjoyed this method of utilizing natural psychic skills?

Crystals In Psychic Work

I'm sure you can easily recall an image of a psychic with a crystal, often seen in TV. The truth is that the good crystal can really help in your own psychic development, so it's another thing that's not just an urban legend.

Theory Behind Crystals

From ancient times, crystals were being associated with magic and psychic abilities, and it hasn't changed yet. What is the connection between crystals and psychic abilities? Generally, crystals can collect and radiate psychic energy. Some of them can gather negative energy from the environment, and some can radiate positive energy. The theory behind this is pretty simple. Specific molecular structure of crystals based on rules of sacred geometry allows them to interact with psychic energy. Energy is the same, but its frequency can be changed by different molecular structures it flows through, in other words - different crystals do different things to psychic energy. That's why some crystals can enhance psychic abilities, while others can heal, and others can help you get rid of a bad mood.

Have you ever paid attention to feelings when fresh snow lies on the ground in winter? Snowflakes is nothing more than ice crystals of frozen water. Then increase the flow of psychic energies during winter time. During the first snow, you can notice the weird pleasant feeling of overwhelming energy around you. This is the psychic energy you feel. The sensations disappear in next few days because your energy body gets used to it and tries to compensate so you won't become distracted or overloaded by these energies.

Quartz And Amethyst

I have experimented with many crystals since I became interested in psychic development. From all my experimentation and personal experiences, and with small help of books and my teachers, I have found out two crystals to be especially useful in psychic work. I'm talking about white, transparent quartz, and amethyst.

Pure white quartz, which is nearly fully transparent, is the most common crystal on Earth. Small quartz can be used to help in focus. Keep a quartz in your hand when meditating or trying psychic readings and you will notice you can focus more easily. Quartz is often used for small kids with ADHD, to keep them calm. In the old days, people used to put a crystal in a bottle of water, and then give water to kids – by drinking, young ones were becoming calmer and less aggressive. Yet, the focus capabilities of quartz is probably the greatest advantage of this crystal every beginner can use. Quartz can just be placed on your desk, or in the room, and it will collect negative energies, so it might be useful for your energetic environment.

Quartz can be also used to help you remember your dreams. Just grab the crystal, and intend it to help you remember your dreams. Then use visualization or intend to break the link with crystal, and place it under the pillow. If you won't remember your dreams after the first night, perform the programming again, and again, until you can really remember the dreams. Of course, remember about keeping a dream journal – it can be helpful not only for enjoying your dreams, but also for discovering new core images for your mind work.

Amethyst, on the other hand, is said to do two things. First, it collects negative energies, so it acts like protective tool. Second, it is said that amethyst helps in developing clairvoyance skills – yet this urban legend has not been confirmed by me yet. What I'm sure of is the first use for amethyst – collecting negative energies; therefore, it's a good idea to keep this crystal in your pocket on a daily basis. Or, you can create an amulet, by changing your amethyst into a pendant, and carry it with you all the time.

Using Crystals

You shouldn't use the same crystal for two or more different purposes. So, if you have a crystal meant to help you remember your dreams, use it for this purpose only; for other purposes, use different crystals. You might end up with a nice set of crystals, one for dreams, one for meditation, one for healing etc. Why is it so important? Because crystals store your intentions – and if you intend the crystal to help you in meditation, it might create problems when used for remembering dreams; or, a crystal meant to protect you against negative energies can be really problematic when used for meditation.

Crystals should be cleansed, as well, at least once a month. It's because they collect different energies within their crystal structure, both positive and negative. And when they're filled with too many 'programs', and negative emotions, they will simple not work at all, or they will work in a negative manner. Cleansing is quite easy.

First, you can just blow the air towards the crystal with the intention to blow all the negativity and unwanted intentions. You can smudge the crystal with incense smoke, or you can hover the crystal above burning candle flame. A nice, working method of cleansing is to bury it in a salt, or in the ground: either in your garden, or in the flowerpot, at least for 24 hours. Finally, you can use water to cleanse the crystal. Try to find a spring or creek of some sort, as water from city water pipes isn't the best choice. Reiki practitioners are often channel Reiki to the crystal, in order to cleanse it. A word of warning, though. Many guidebooks and psychic teachers, or crystal workers, might tell you to use sunlight to cleanse the crystals. Sufficient to say, this knowledge is an effect of misleading New Age propaganda, if I may say that. The truth is that no crystal enjoy sunlight. In reality, sunlight destroys the crystal structure, so you won't be cleansing your crystals, rather you will be destroying them. Do not use sunlight, nor moonlight for crystals cleansing.

World Of Skeptic

If there's a light side, there must be also a dark side of the Force. Sooner or later you will face the problem of skepticism. It is hard to tell if we, as psychic practitioners are the good guys, or the bad guys, but everyone knows that if there's a psychic, there must be also a skeptic. Of course, it's too general, but we will get into details in just a moment. For now, you must know that by entering the world of paranormal phenomena as an energy worker, you're also at the same time entering our little war between believers and skeptics, because of this you must prepare yourself. But what you might not know is that it's important for psychic practitioner to be a skeptic, too.

Skeptic And Pseudoskeptic

Skeptic is not a person that doesn't believe in psychic phenomena or anything paranormal. Skeptic is a person that is careful of what he or she believes in, he doesn't believe because someone told him, in order to believe, he must learn, and he does that by doing research and experiments on his own - he must see with his eyes, and feel with his palms, in other worlds - he needs proofs. But when he finally gets them, he becomes a believer - but not because he heard it's true, instead he saw the proofs.

But beside skeptics, there are also so-called pseudoskeptics out there. Those are people who do not care about proofs, they don't even care about the truth - what they care about is their own point of view that need to be saved from people like us, and their point of view is clear: "no matter what, I don't care - what I say is the truth, what you say is false and you're one big fraud". Pseudoskeptics think this way and only this way, because they can't accept that someone's point of view might be the reality, and they are the ones who are wrong.

Scientific Ways To Deal With Skeptic

Forget about dealing with pseudo-skeptics. They won't change their minds. Proving them anything is like trying to open an eyes of a blind person – no matter what you do, the blind won't see. He just can't. Focus on dealing with real open-minded skeptics. Even when you're talking about your own psychic abilities, then it's good to start with explaining that psychic phenomena is the real deal. The most popular way people try to debunk all your psychic or paranormal claims is to say that "there are no proofs, the scientific world says it's impossible". Fortunately for us, those skeptics are wrong and there's a lot of scientific proofs to prove the reality of psychic phenomena. You can easily defend yourself by reminding people and mentioning the following:

- Stanford Research Institute research on psychical phenomena. There were hundreds if not thousands of research on Remote Viewing, telepathy, precognition and psychometry, not mentioning psychokinesis there. Most of which were sponsored by the US government, by the way.
- Rhine Research Center does store a lot of documents about real psychic and paranormal experiences, and their archives are filled with date from Zener and

Ganzfeld experiments (don't forget to explain people how does these experiments looked like).
- Organizations like Society for Psychical Research from the United Kingdom have collected a lot of date in over 100 years of existence, as well as performed a lot of experiments in very scientific conditions, and they continue to work for this very day.

It is a common way to debunk scientific claims by mentioning they've been performed by amateurs, but as you can see, Stanford Research Institute or Rhine Research Center aren't very amateur, are they? In most cases the above tips to deal with skeptics works, because skeptics do not have any way to deny the scientific research.

But are skeptics really to be persuaded? Sometimes I do not think so, and personally, I do not waste my time persuading anyone. It is my belief that skeptics will open their eyes when they're ready. From my current standpoint, I believe that belief in reality of psychic phenomena is an element of inner evolution of mind – and our capability of understanding that the world is something more than just a bunch of atoms. Because of this, a word of advice – do not try to persuade anyone about reality of psychic phenomena if you don't have to. Don't think it's your mission to persuade people, don't think that you're any different from thousands of psychics and energy workers who ever tried fighting with skeptics. Just focus on your own growth, and that should be enough. After all, it's your life, and you want the same thing we all want – to be happy. Fighting with skeptics is not a path to happiness. Trust me. Been there, done that, bought the t-shirt.

The problem of the modern world and skeptics is simple. Skeptics believe, with nearly religious fanaticism, that logic and rational thinking are the only proper way to perceive the world.

And they think that anyone, who don't see the world as they do, is either fraud, or lunatic. People have created themselves a world full of technology, yet without the soul. But don't worry about that. After all, you have found your soul, and you're exploring what was supposed to be impossible.

How To Be An Open-minded Skeptic

It is an irony, because if you want to deal with psychics, you must learn how to be a skeptic, a real open-minded skeptic yourself. Because if you remain a bit skeptical, it will be harder for others to fool you. And trust me, there are countless, useless sources, techniques, systems and knowledge fields regarding the supernatural. If you want to grow, you can't accept every single psychical theory out there. There are some rules you should stick to if you want to remain skeptical, yet open-mind at the same time.

- **Never assume someone is lying** - when your friend is telling you that he moved a cola can with psychokinesis, do not assume he is lying, maybe he did move the can with PK? You're the man, go and see if your friend can repeat the phenomena
- **Never assume you're right** - maybe you are wrong, and others are right; more important, you can't be right all over the time, maybe right now you're wrong?
- **Never assume that what expert says is the truth** - even experts can be wrong; also, there are different kinds of experts. Is the "expert" a scientist, or maybe just a spiritual guru?
- **Always look for good proofs** - if you're practicing on your own psychic development, it's simple; but when researching the subject and looking for proofs elsewhere, remember to look for good proofs.

Information given by people aren't proofs, but captured video of cola tin being moved with psychokinesis might be a proof, but might not be a proof good enough - it is easy to fake it. Be skeptical...

- **Look for witnesses** - has anyone else saw the phenomena? Look for such people and analyze information given by them, are they the same or are they different from each other?
- **Experiment on your own** - finally, if you want to learn psychics you have to experiment on your own - try different techniques, systems, and exercises. When stumbling upon interesting report of someone's experiment, try to repeat it, maybe you'll be able to do so and you'll learn something by this.

But don't push too much – keep an open mind, and remember, that many psychic truths are spiritual truths, as well. And as such, some truths and experiences cannot be proved with our western, logical thinking. It's just impossible – it's like trying to apply the laws of physics to explain the phenomena of love. If you can't believe something, and you can't persuade yourself to believe something, then get over it. Move on, and know that maybe one day, you will understand. Do not create attachments to things you do not understand, do not force yourself to research things you don't believe in unless you have strong exploration and adventurous tendencies. As I said, some spiritual truths require more spiritual mind to understand. And one day, you might understand them.

Specialization

At the beginning of this book, I have mentioned that sometimes, during your psychic development, you might awake your psychic gifts. Somehow, this relates to another thing I want to mention – specialization of a psychic. The problem many beginners face is that you can't learn everything in a practical way. There is just too much to learn and study. Sure, you can have wide theoretical knowledge, but in reality in practical aspects, you need to choose. That's why specialization matters. And that's something I encourage you to do - focus on few skills, and don't worry about the rest.

Perhaps you think you might need all these skills - but why? It's much better option to master two skills, and find other psychics who have mastered other skills - this way, by forming a "team" you all have access to more nicely developed skills, that you wouldn't be able to develop on your own. Keep this in mind my friend, focus is the essence of mastering skills. What is more, even if you want to learn two or three skills only, don't try to do this at once. Learn one skill first - focus on in for few months. By turning all your attention to learning this particular skill, you can master it much faster than those who try to learn few things at the same time. When this particular skill will be mastered, you will be able to move further and master another skill. Perhaps when you will be learning fast enough, you will learn more than three or four skills.

I know psychic readers, who give intuitive readings regarding spiritual growth, financial issues, health and relationship problems. I know psychic healers, who do not practice psychic readings, but can support healing of many illnesses. I know mediums who help spirits move to the light, but they can't do psychic healing. I could post many of such examples. The point is – you don't have to do everything. You can become an expert in a small area of psychic phenomena, just like you can't be a doctor, physicist, designer, writer, publisher and engineer at the same time. You need to choose.

You might want to use your psychic abilities in your normal work, in business, family life. You might want to become professional psychic reader, or you might want to use your psychic skills in archeology. What I want to say is that you don't have to see spirits and ghosts to be psychic; you don't have to give psychic readings to be psychic. In reality, being psychic is about tapping into your intuition, and learning how to use it for different purposes. But these purposes, your ultimate goal, is only yours to choose. You can use psychic abilities in different areas of your life that doesn't seem very psychic. And when you do, and when you accept that you don't have to learn everything, you will make a great progress. Because thinking that you should learn every single psychic skill that exists, will only block your true development.

I openly admit that I do use help of other psychics – I can't see spirits, and if I would have to send a spirit to the light, I would ask my friend, Tom, to do so. When I have problems with my own core images which I cannot deal with because they're so 'powerful', I ask my spiritual teacher for help. When I need additional intuitive counseling, I know who to talk with. Don't be afraid to ask other psychics for help if you have to. You can master one skill, and others will ask for your help, as well. You can master one skill and be very good at it, so others won't have to learn this skill on their own. This way, we create a huge psychic community. Everyone is special, and the only thing that connect us is the fact that we're more aware of the psychic world right in front of us.

How To Use Psychic Abilities In Daily Life

Psychic abilities wouldn't be useful if they would be needed only on occasion, or for pure psychic work. As psychic practitioner, you would like to use psychic abilities on a daily basis. For such people like you, here are some ideas for practical ways to use psychic skills.

Maybe you would like to help people - give them psychic readings from time to time? Often, people need advices or answers to their questions. A psychic can provide such supernatural support using his or her skills. Or you can experiment with psychic healing - people get ill often these days, why not using psychic energies to improve their condition?

You can also help yourself - you can seek advices with personal psychic readings, just by listening to your intuition or psychic impressions you're picking up. Or you can use energy work to improve your healing rate if you get ill. My personal record is healing a cold within two days without any medicine, why normally I was getting better within no less than six days, taking medicines at the same time. See the difference? In order to speed up the healing process, classic energy work (energy drawing techniques) can be applied.

You can make money - from both psychic readings and psychic healing, but you can also try to use different Extra-Sensory Perception skills to find out numbers for lottery or choose the best deal in your job. Wait, lottery? You might think "if it's really possible, then why psychics aren't rich?" - well, first of all, you don't know if they're not rich. Second of all, if I would be winning money on lottery thanks to my psychics skills, I wouldn't admit that...

Extra-Sensory Perception, as I already mentioned, can be used for making choices - in job, relationship, even in the local store to find out if the food you're about to buy is a healthy choice, or which road should you choose to avoid traffic jam. I'm sure that you can think of many ways, in which you can use your psychic intuition.

And you can use energy work and sensing capabilities - for example when meeting new people, to find out if you two will have a good relationship with each other. Or you can scan a new flat you're about to buy and find out how you feel inside it, if it's the right place for you to live in.

You can try to make a living with your psychic abilities. You can participate in psychic archeology and seek buried archaeological sites. Or you can explore the subject of radionics and dowsing - to find water for building wells, or for consulting people choosing a place to build their house. Finally, you can simple give psychic readings for money, or organize psychic training courses in your nearest area.

As you can see, psychic abilities aren't very far from reality, and they can be used in many ways on a daily basis. I believe it's your imagination that limits you. Don't be afraid of using your psychic abilities for things that don't seem to be very 'spiritual' or 'psychic'. Your skills should be used to improve your life – keep this in mind.

The World Of Spirits

You're never alone, even if you sit down in an empty room. I don't want to scare you, as there's not much to be afraid of, but we're constantly surrounded by spirits. Some people can see them, and some can't. Perhaps during your psychic development, you will open your Third Eye wide enough to perceive spirits through your 'physical' eye. But for now, know this – around you, there are countless spirits. For example, trees, parks, and even flats and houses are full of nature spirits. They are nice creatures, but do not disturb their peace – when angry, they can be really nasty.

Of course, there are also haunted places, where earthbound spirits exist. Maybe you will specialize in mediumship, and spirit releasement one day, and you will be helping these spirits to move to the light.

There are also angels – spiritual beings described in many sacred books. They are the guardians, teachers and... more. One of the types of angels is called 'spirit guide'. And every person has such spirit guide.

Your Spirit Guide

A spirit guide – a disembodied entity that is always there with them, giving advices and sharing knowledge. I'm sure you can recall few books or mainly TV shows with psychics discussing or just mentioning their spirit guides. Personally I admit, that I had at least one spirit guide in the past. His name was Henry, and he was probably more freaked out than me, with specific ironic, and sometimes sarcastic sense of humor. But if you don't want to, there's no need to look for your own guide, or even believe in his presence (or her presence, spirit guide might be female). I guess being aware of a spirit guide is more related to spiritual growth and needs, than pure psychic development.

How To Discover Your Spirit Guide

It's not necessary for psychic development, but if you want to find out your own spirit guide that might give you a lot of advices regarding psychic development, here's a practical tutorial to do so.

There are no fireworks for this. Simple sit down and fall into a meditative state - it doesn't have to be a deep trance, just clear your mind and focus. When you're relaxed and focused enough, ask "are you here" - with the intend to direct this message to your spirit guide. After you ask the question, wait for an answer. You might hear a "whisper" in your head, but that's very, very rare. Greater possibility is that you will just "know" the answer, just like any other psychic impression. Or you might pick up a thought in your mind, that's not very yours.

When you get the answer or impression, ask another question - "what is your name" - and wait for an answer. Make sure you hear the answer correctly and you're done. Honestly, there's no other way to find your spirit guide. You ask the question and wait for an answer. But along with your development, your guide might appear to you in a different way – maybe as the song on the radio. Or maybe, one day you might even see your guide.

With time, you will learn what are your thoughts, and what are psychic impressions generated by your spirit guide. You will know his or her thoughts, and you will engage in very active conversation from time to time. In the end, you will find out that communicating with your spirit guide is like chatting with your physical friend - the difference is, you might not see your guide for your entire life.

Just remember - true spirit guide will never ask you or tell you to do something evil. And very often, he won't make choices for you. A guide act mainly as a consultant, it's you who have to make the final decision. In any way, through your spirit guide you might receive guidance and intuitive thoughts. But again, if you don't want to seek your spirit guide, you don't have to. Your intuition will work anyway.

Channeling

Quite popular ability these days, channeling is an ability to channel messages from spirit entities. It's quite popular, and you can easily find thousands of channeled books and wisdom from higher planes of existence, available on the market. But personally, I do not suggest practicing channeling if you haven't spent at least 30 years working with psychic forces. You never know who's on the other side, and you don't know the value of channeled information, really. You don't know if you're channeling wisdom, or faked information meant to create another cult. Trust me, there are astral entities out there who aren't nice and pleasant, and they seek worshipers to feed with psychic energies.

For this reason, I rarely trust any channeled messages, and if I receive such, I try to cross-reference them with other sources, like ancient Taoist or Buddhist texts, or consult them with my teacher and psychic friends. No light entity will ask you to create a cult or sect, and worship it. No light entity will tell you that you're "next Avatar with glorious mission". No light entity will tell you that you suffer because of the pain of Mother Earth.

Beware of channeled messages, and be skeptical about them. If they sound reasonable and positive, and your trust the source (for example, the message comes from your spirit guide that never let you down), consider trusting the message. But don't be paranoid, either. Your spirit guide can share a lot of useful info with you. But, again, he or she won't try to create another cult.

Now, you might ask, what is the difference between channeled message, spirit guide message, and intuitive message? Well, the difference is so subtle that it cannot be described with words. At least not until you can use advanced clairaudience, or until you can physically see the spirit that is channeling the message. I will say it this way: with time and practice, you will learn how to distinct intuition, spirit guide and other messages. It's just a matter of practice.

The Book Of Exercises

The most popular question I'm being asked when talking about developing psychic abilities is "how can I develop these skills further". My answer is simple - practice, practice, practice. Practice makes perfection.

Continue energy work and meditation, and practice psychic skills daily. For example, you can go to a mall and try to sense the difference in psychic energies and people psychic signatures. Or you can go to a museum and practice psychometry. Look for people who would like to get a free psychic reading and enjoy this process.

Continue to create psiballs. Ground, center and shield on a daily basis. If you look around, you can find many ways to use the tutorials from this book day by day. You also need some more active ways to develop psychic abilities on a daily basis. Because of this, I've prepared a set of simple exercises you can practice daily, and by this - develop your psychic skills further each day.

Energy Pulsing

For this exercise, you need a practice partner. Energy pulsing game will teach you how to both send and receive energies (therefore, how to sense it, too) - both skills are the basic energy work skills everyone should practice.

Belows is a step by step tutorial for energy pulsing exercise.

- **Sit down and relax** – Sit down facing your partner and relax. One of you will be sending pulses, and the other one will be sensing them. Choose the person who will pulse first. Place one of your hands facing each other with palms, leaving an inch of free space between palms. Personally I use my left hand to pulse and sense because it's more sensitive to psychic energies.
- **Ground and Center** – Now that you sit and your hands are ready, both of you have to ground and center. You already know how to do this, so I won't repeat myself.
- **Pulse the energy** – Now the person that pulse first have to move the energy from the Lower Tan T'ien and

move it into the hand – gather the energy in your hand for few seconds, then push it outside, directing it towards hand of your partner.
- **Sense the energy** – If you're the person that sense the energy, while centered you have to pay attention to all weird or "different than normal" physical feelings you get in your hand. Personally when the energy is directed towards my hand, I sense it as something pushing my hand, or as electric impulse moving through it. When you sense the psychic energy, say it aloud so your partner you confirm or deny the pulse.

And that's basically it. Pulser is continuing to make pulses, while senser is sensing them. If the pulse took place and senser said it aloud that he felt something, pulser should confirm or deny the fact of pulse. Try to make pulses irregular, so they will be harder to guess.

You can even make this game more entertaining if you will play for score.

Crystals Sensing

If you do not have a practice partner, you can use crystals to develop energy sensing abilities further. Below is another tutorial.

- **Prepare crystals** – First you need some crystals, from 3 to 5. Use different crystals, for beginners I suggest using amethyst, quartz and mahogany obsidian. If you don't have any crystals, look around, you might find a store for mineral collectors or you can try both Amazon and eBay. When you have crystals, place them on the table in front of you, keep about 5 inches of space

between crystals, so they won't interfere with each other.
- **Warm up your hand** – Now you have to use New Energy Ways to warm up your hand. Imagine (using tactile visualization, meaning – feel physical sensations) the energy spinning in your hand, like a vortex. Do this for about 15 seconds or even few minutes if you're a beginner in energy work. Your hand should be warmed up by now.
- **Start sensing by moving your hand above crystals** – Hover your hand above first crystal, close your eyes and pay attention to all sensations. If you don't feel anything, spin the energy like in the previous step again for few seconds and again, focus and pay attention. What do you feel? Heat, cold, tingling, pressure, anything physical?
- **Move forward** – Focus on single crystal for a minute or so, then move to another crystal and again pay attention to all your physical sensations. Then move to another crystal and start over from the beginning. Each time focus for a minute and pay attention to physical feelings.

This way you will learn how different crystals radiate with psychic energies and it will be a good way to develop energy sensing. Experiment with different crystals, notice the feelings, notice the differences between them. At first you might not be able to sense much, but with time, you will learn what to look for when it comes to psychic sensing, so be patient.

Cards Sensing

This exercise will help you develop Extra-Sensory Perception skills. You're going to play a form of "memory".

- **Grab a deck of cards** - From the deck, choose up to four pairs of cards, for example, two queens, two kings, two ace, two fours. Divide these eight cards into two small decks, each one of them should contain one cards of it's kind, so each deck will contain one queen, one king, one ace and one four.
- **Put the cards on the table** - Put first deck on the left, and second deck on the right - with the bottom (side with images) facing down the table, and each cards alone, with few centimeters of space between them. This way, you will have two opposite decks on two sides of the table, and simple access to each cards.
- **Pick up one card** - Choose the hand that is going to sense the cards, and pick up single random card from the opposite deck. So, if you will use your left hand to do sensing, choose the card from the right deck.
- **Sense the card** - Your task is to turn the same two cards in both decks. So if, in the right deck, you have chosen, for example, a queen, you need to sense the queen in the other deck. Hover your hand above the first card of the left deck and notice how does it feel. The right card should be warmer than others. Hover your hand on all cards and try to sense the right one. Act on your first impression, if you believe that "this is the card", just turn it over and see if you're right.

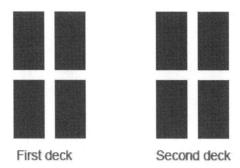

Illustration 8: That's how you should place the cards

With this exercise, you can practice on your own without any practice partner.

Energy Sensing and Gathering

There is one more exercise to practice energy sensing. For this exercise, you're going to need a practice partner.

- **Sit down and relax** - Both of you should ground and center. While sitting, face each other in proximity. Choose the person that is going to gather the energy in hands, and the person that is going to sense the energies.
- **Gather the energy** - The gatherer should use New Energy Ways to gather the energy in one of this palms - choose the palm randomly, so the senser won't know which hand is going to be charged with energies

- **Sense the energy** - The senser should sense which palm is charged. Expand your energy field to cover the hands of your partner - you can use either simple visualization, or New Energy Ways and tactile visualization. The hand that is charged should be felt, for example, as pressure, or "something in your field" that doesn't feels right.

And that's it - it's a simple energy manipulation exercise that will help you with your sensing abilities.

Moving Further

You have learned energy manipulation: you can create a psychic shield, psiballs, perform psychic reading and psychometry, maybe you can also perform psychic healing. You have learned how to unleash your intuition, and how to use it for different purposes. Now all you have to do is to look for new opportunities, so you can practise your abilities.

In the end, you will understand one thing - that all that energy work, visualization, programming, thinking process etc. is pointless. Because the only thing that you really need, is your intention.

This will be realized at some point - not at first, because your subconscious might cause problems regarding this, so you won't trust your intentions truly, and you will think (subconsciously), that you require visualization. At some point, you will just be blessed with understanding, and you will re-program your mind, so your psychic skills will operate only on your intentions.

When you will realize it, all the techniques of psiball creation, or psychic reading, or psychometry etc. will become just ideas generators, showing you the way things work. Think about it this way - at first, you visualize the energy that connects you to the person for the purpose of psychic reading. At some point, you realize that the only thing you need is your intention. From that moment on, you will be just thinking about things, and you will get instant connection, instant psychic input, and then you will instantly break links. The energy work will be going on, but it won't be conscious any more. It will happen in the background, governed by your subconscious mind. The whole point behind learning different techniques, and step by step tutorials is to re-program your mind, unlearn what you have learned, and learn new things.

Practice is important, it's the only way you can keep learning. Through practice, you learn how to use your intentions instead of step-by-step techniques. Through practice, you learn new symbols that your mind provides you with during psychic work, and you expand your personal dictionary of psychic symbols and their meanings. Through practice, you deal with more core images, and you improve your energetics, and through this, you improve your health and psychic abilities. And you learn the greatest secrets of psychic phenomena: that you can shape your life as you want it and that you're never alone, there always is guidance, that mystical power looking over you.

Do not rush - the world of psychic phenomena is dangerous for total newbies. But with time, you will learn more and more, and the more you learn, the more you understand. The more you understand, the safer, and more effective psychic worker you are.

Finally, more than anything, remember to trust your intuition and guidance of the Source. Psychics are channels of the greater force. We help ourselves and then, we help others. Finally, through our group effort, we help the entire world, and the entire mankind. It might be too much for you. But remember, even the smallest difference, the smallest help, can have huge effects.

Summary of the book

You have reached the end of this book. Hopefully, you followed it step by step, and you have your energy body developed, and chakras opened. I hope that Psychic Development Simplified became important resource for your further studies and exploration of psychic phenomena.

Developing energy body, opening chakras and learning psychic techniques is a huge step each person's life, but it's just the first step. Your journey has just begun, and there's a long way you must walk. But you will not be alone. Now open your eyes and start walking. And as always - have fun and enjoy! Your journey has only just begun!

Thanks for reading!

Make a note in your journal

Look at the first note in your journal that you wrote few months ago. Read it over, and think about it. How big progress did you make? What skills have you learned? How did your perception changed since that time?

Read over all your notes, and enjoy weird experiences you had – they're proofs for your developing psychic abilities. Continue your development, and one year from now return to this note – and see how greater progress you have made.

Resources

Within this additional section, I included bibliography and further reading, a training schedule, on-line resources, and glossary of terms. I hope it will be useful for all of you.

Schedule

It's time to put things together in a training schedule and learn few additional things. In addition to all sections of this book, here is a simple schedule that will give you the better understanding of timetable.

Time	Things to do	Additional information
0-2 weeks	Initial exercises	Play around and test your initial psychic skills; learn how to meditate; learn terminology and basic theory;
0-3 months	Mind Work	Work with meditation, affirmations and emotional healing;

3-10 months	Energy Body Development	Solely focus on energy body development and learn the theory about the energy system and energy manipulation;
10-12 months	Opening Chakras	Start opening all 7 chakras; at the same time, continue with drawing energy 15 minutes each day
From the 10th month	Psiball	Practice making psiballs for another month
From the 8th month	Practice of psychic techniques	Start learning specific psychic techniques;
12th month and further	Further exploration	Read, explore and learn more from other resources while continuing energy work and techniques practice;

On-line reading

Below is a list of useful resources you can access on-line that might expand your knowledge about psychics and psychic phenomena.

- **http://astateofmind.eu** - My blog where I teach how to develop psychic abilities. Read it if you want to explore the subject of psychics further, and get additional tips and techniques for developing psychic abilities.

- **http://PsiPog.net** - one of the oldest websites about psychics, the one that created the OPC.
- **http://www.remoteviewdaily.com/**– Try your remote viewing skills on a daily basis. This site provides you with free remote viewing target, each day new.

Send feedback & comments

If you have found this workbook and training system useful, I will appreciate any comments and feedback emails, and testimonials or reviews, as well – simple send them to my email: nathan@astateofmind.eu

Network with the author on Facebook:
http://facebook.com/astateofmindblog!

About the Author

Nathaniel is psychic and Reiki practitioner. On his website, A State of Mind, he educate about psychic development and psychic abilities, and he also provides psychic services, mainly related to helping others in their own psychic growth. He lives in Poland, and when he's not writing, or blogging, or teaching, he study paranormal phenomena mysteries.

You can learn more here: http://astateofmind.eu/about/

Glossary of Terms

Aura View - An ability to perceive psychic energy field around living beings.

Analytical Overlay - Known also as Frontloading, it is experiencing something what one is expecting to experience, rather than experiencing something that is actually there. Using simpler language, experiencing things you want to experience even if what you're experiencing is not real.

Centering - Finding inner peace, a private, personal part within yourself, it might be called a form of meditation. It is used to calm down during stress, or psychic overloads. Some psychics refer to "The Zone", or "The Temple" as I call it. It is an imaginary place within your mind, which is your private sanctuary. Such place is a method of visual support for centering meditation.

Chakras - Based on Hindu beliefs, within your energy system, chakras are your energy centers, visualized as spinning circles of psychic energies. There are seven main chakras, and thousands of smaller spread all across your body. Chakras are important in psychic development, as they are the way to focus and manipulate psychic energies.

Energy Body - Also known as an energy system, is a complex structure of Chakras, Nadises and Tan T'iens, and it's meant to store, utilise, and use psychic energies.

Extra-Sensory Perception - A set of psychic skills that allows to acquire information without using normal five physical sense.

Filtering - An expanded skill of grounding, when you get rid of old, negative energies and draw new, fresh energy into your energy system

Flaring - An ability to make energy constructs visible.

Grounding - An ability used to release psychic energies from the energy system into the ground, as means of field maintenance.

LTT - LTT stands for Lower Tan T'ien, lower, one of three energy storage centers within energy body.

MBA - Tactile visualization system that utilise physical feelings to manipulate psychic energies.

Meridian, See: Nadis, The

Nadis, the Nadis - (a Hindu term) is an energy channel within your energy system. There are three main Nadis's (left – Pingala, right – Ida and the central, spine – Shushumna), and thousands smaller channels, all responsible for transporting psychic energies throughout your body. Visualizing psychic energies within Nadis's greatly help the energy manipulation abilities.

New Energy Ways - Energy manipulation system developed by Robert Bruce that focuses on manipulating energy using tactile visualization called Mobile Body Awareness.

Psiball- Psiball is the most basic energy construct. Simply, it is a ball of psychic energy, which can be used to perform different tasks (using construct programming), but mainly it is used for basic energy manipulation training.

Psychic Reading - An ability to perceive information via psychic means regarding living people.

Psychometry - An ability to perceive information via psychic means from physical objects.

Shield, psychic shield - Psychic shield is an energy construct in a shape of bubble created around your body and aura (your energy field). It's primary function is to protect your from outer energies, and to protect the world from your own energies you want to keep inside (such as unintentional telepathy broadcasting, or poltergeist activity). There is only one type/kind of the shield, but the there are dozen methods of creating and programming it. Some psychics have problems with creating even a basic one, some are protected by shield with multiple levels, and some are protected by so one-level shield so powerful that nothing can pass it.

Clairaudience - It is an ability to hear voices of ghosts, spirits and energy entities. The reason why psychic can hear spirit voice in his own language (i.e. English) might be related to the fact that most information are stored within psychic energies being transferred to psychic's mind, and the capabilities of it to "translate" information stored within energies into human language. Also, it might be related to the fact that language is just the representation of thoughts, but thoughts are always the same.

Clairvoyance - It is an ability to see ghosts, spirits and energy entities, either as mist, fields of light or "flesh & blood" person. As in clairaudience, it might be related to the fact that psychic mind has the ability to "translate" information about visual signals stored within psychic energies into more "realistic" signal.

Empathy- Empathy is an ability to feel other people's emotions as if they were your own. Usually a person learns it automatically along with energy manipulation.

Precognition - An ability to see into the future, i.e. in your dreams. It's not a rare ability, and it might become a very often occurrence as you'll be developing your psychic skills further.

Shelling- An ability to make another layer for psychic construct meant to hold first layer together.

Scanning- It is a process of acquiring information about the person or entity, or even place and object (psychometry) from its energy fields (i.e. aura), by use of psychic means.

Tactile Imagining - A form of visualization and energy manipulation, when you physically feel the psychic energies.

Ward - A construct made of psychic energy, meant to perform a specific task, for example, repel astral beings.

Bibliography and further reading

Acorah, D. *The Psychic World of Derek Acorah: Discover How to Develop Your Hidden Powers.* Piatkus Books 2005.

Brown, J. *Playful Psychic.* Online Access: <http://psipog.net/activepsy/> 1993.

Bruce, R. *Energy Work: The Secret of Healing and Spiritual Development.* Hampton Roads Pub Co 2007.

Bruce, R. *Practical Psychic Self-Defence. Understanding and Surviving Unseen Influences.* Hampton Roads Pub Co 2002.

Connelly, S. M. *The Psion's Handbook: Overview of psychics.* Online Access: <http://psipog.net/ebook.html> 2001.

Du Tertre, N. *Psychic Intuition.* Create Space 2010.

Hewitt, W. *Psychic Development for Beginners: An easy guide to releasing and developing your psychic abilities.* Llewellyn Publications 1996.

Katz, D.L. *Extraordinary Psychic: Proven Techniques to Master Your Natural Psychic Abilities.* Llewellyn Publications 2008.

Katz, D. L. *You Are Psychic: The Art of Clairvoyant Reading & Healing.* Llewellyn Publications 2004.

Morehouse, D. A. *Remote Viewing: The Complete User's Manual for Coordinate Remote Viewing.* Sounds True 2007.

Ward, T. *Discover your Psychic Powers: A practical guide to psychic development & spiritual growth.* Book Sales 2000.

Żądło, L. *Jak korzystać ze zdolności parapsychicznych.* Ravi 1994.

Żądło, L. *Rozwijanie zdolności parapsychicznych.* Randall & Sfinks 1993.

Wojciech 'Nathaniel' Usarzewicz

Psychic Development Simplified

Made in the USA
Middletown, DE
20 February 2017